FORD ESCORT
REPAIRS

FORD ESCORT REPAIRS

by

B. C. MacDONALD

*(Author of "Car Doctor A-Z",
"Car Repairs Properly Explained",
"BLMC Mini Repairs",
"BLMC 1100 and 1300 Repairs",
"Morris Minor 1000 Repairs",
and "Ford Cortina Repairs")*

PAPERFRONTS

ELLIOT RIGHT WAY BOOKS
KINGSWOOD, SURREY, U.K.

PREFACE

The purpose of this book is to help the Escort owner reduce the cost of motoring by helping him to do some of the repairs himself and generally to provide the information that will enable him to maintain the car in good condition.

The aim has been to give the maximum amount of information in the space available.

The Author's thanks are due to different departments of the Ford Motor Co. Ltd. for supplying essential information and for allowing the use of illustrations. The book is, however, in no way sponsored by the manufacturers.

Thanks are also due to Joseph Lucas Ltd. who supplied various illustrations associated with their products.

Other titles by B. C. MacDonald

CAR DOCTOR A–Z (SYMPTOMS-CAUSES-CURES)
The unique A.B.C. fault-finder for all cars.

CAR REPAIRS PROPERLY EXPLAINED
Covers maintenance and how cars work—lots of general information for beginners.

TRACE AND REPAIR YOUR CAR ELECTRICAL FAULTS
Your guide to becoming a car electrical fault tracing mastermind.

BLMC MINI REPAIRS

BLMC 1100/1300 REPAIRS

FORD CORTINA REPAIRS

Each uniform with this volume

CONTENTS

ILLUSTRATIONS

1
The Engine

1.1 General

The first range of Escorts included 2 and 4 door saloons, the estate car and the van, available with various qualities of trim and extra fitments and basically having a choice of two engine sizes, the 1100 or the 1300. The additional label L, XL, GT or SPORT denoted the standard of trim. Automatic transmission could be fitted to all models having the larger engine except the GT and SPORT models. There were also three high performance models *not covered by this book,* the Twin Cam, the RS 1600 and the Mexico.

The Escort II range adds the Popular and the Popular Plus at the inexpensive end of the range with choice of 1100 or 1300 engine. Next up the line are the 1100 or 1300 L's, followed by the 1300 GL. In addition there is a 1300 SPORT and a larger engined 1600 SPORT and a 1300 GHIA or a 1600 GHIA. Automatic transmission is available at option with the 1300 engine or the 1600 engine where available.

About 23 items of optional equipment are available including servo brakes, remote control door mounted rear view mirror, automatic transmission, hazard warning flashers, rear fog lamp, tinted glass, halogen headlights, over-riders, laminated windscreen.

All the engines are vertical in line water cooled four stroke cycle units with push rod operated overhead valves. Each has a five bearing crankshaft, "Bowl in Piston" combustion chambers and a cross flow cylinder head.

1.2 Fault Symptoms
  (1) Engine lacks power.
  (2) Engine overheats.
  (3) Engine will not start.
  (4) Engine starts with difficulty.

(5) Engine tends to die out when accelerating.
(6) Engine knocks.
(7) There is a clicking sound when the engine is running.
(8) Compression is poor.
(9) Exhaust smokes heavily.
(10) Engine uses too much oil.
(11) Engine uses too much petrol.
(12) Engine misfires.
(13) Engine stalls—will not idle.
(14) Engine idles too fast.
(15) Engine runs erratically.
(16) Engine runs on wide throttle only.
(17) Engine squeaks.
(18) Engine backfires.
(19) Engine seizes—locks solid.

1.3 Causes and Cures

(1) This may be due to general wear or to lack of tune. The engine will not continue to run efficiently unless it is properly maintained. Sufficient wear to affect the performance of an engine would only take place over a large mileage. The first effect is usually cylinder bore and piston ring wear (see 1.6, p. 24). Eventually bearing wear becomes evident by knocking sounds. These faults can only be rectified by major overhaul or by fitting a replacement engine.

If the cause of the trouble is simply lack of tune, this can be put right by fitting a new set of plugs with properly adjusted gaps or by having the old plugs serviced (see 4.40, p. 86). Make sure the high tension (plug and coil) leads are sound. The leads should be clean and free from chafing; dirt on the leads may cause leakage. If there is any sign of deterioration renew all the leads.

Excessive carbon deposit in the engine will result in loss of power, but pinking (metallic tinkling heard while engine is under load) would indicate the source of the trouble.

Poor compression in one or more cylinders will cause the trouble (see 1.12, p. 28). One or more cylinders may not be firing. To check, have the engine running at tick-over speed and pull the lead off one of the plugs. This puts this particular cylinder out of action and if it was firing before the lead was removed the change in the running of the engine will be obvious. If removing the lead makes no difference this proves that the cylinder was not firing. Replace the lead on the plug and successively remove and replace all the leads of all the plugs. In this way the faulty cylinder will be found, and the fault must be due to the plug (see 4.40, p. 86), or to a shorting high tension lead; therefore examine the lead carefully for this fault.

The ignition timing may be retarded, but this would cause overheating (see 4.49, p. 90) or it may be too far advanced which would cause knocking (see (6) below).

Check that the brakes are not binding, especially the handbrake (see 7.4, p. 116 and 7.7, p. 117). The trouble could be a carburettor fault (see 2.2, p. 34). Overheating due to a weak mixture at the carburettor will cause loss of power. Overheating may also be caused by an ignition fault (see 4.38, p. 81) or by lack of oil.

Check also the cooling system (see 3.2, p. 48).

(2) This may be a carburettor fault, (see 2.2, p. 34) or an ignition fault (see 4.38, p. 81). It may be caused by lack of oil (see 1.14, p. 29), lack of water, or by binding brakes (see 7.2, p. 114). The fan belt may be slipping or broken.

(3) This is usually an ignition fault (see 4.38, p. 81). It may be a carburation fault (see 2.2, p. 34). If the two likely causes are not to blame there may be a mechanical fault, a broken timing chain (valves not operating), or loss of compression (see 1.12, p. 28).

(4) Usually caused by an ignition or carburettor fault (see (3) above).

(5) This is a carburation or fuel fault (see chapter 2).

(6) Make sure that the knock is in the engine. If the knock is only heard when the car is moving it is somewhere in the car or transmission, and the first check should be for a loose wheel. With the car stopped depress the accelerator once or twice to raise the engine speed slightly. If the knock is in the engine its frequency will rise and fall with the engine speed. Note if the sound of the knock has the same frequency as the 'speed' of the engine or is lower. The valve gear runs at half engine speed and any knock in it can be located by this speed difference.

A knock can often be located by feel. When the engine is running at tick-over speed put your hand on the dynamo; any knock in the dynamo will be immediately evident. But MIND the fan! Keep your hands well clear of it. Feel the distributor and other parts of the engine. In this way a knock can often be located.

The ear provides a sensitive means of locating knocks. It is possible to buy stethoscopes similar to those used by doctors for use in knock detection. A simple but effective one can be made quite easily. Take a piece of half inch wood rod about a yard long and fit one end with a piece of convex shaped round wood. The ear is rested on the curved surface while the other end of the rod is pressed into contact with various parts of the engine. The noise will become louder as the source is approached and can thus be located.

Check the fan. Are the blades touching anything as they rotate? Sometimes a worn fan belt will throw off a loose piece of material which causes a knock by hitting something as it moves.

Worn big end bearings rattle and clatter when the engine is running without load (idling) but when pulling under load the noise tends to disappear. To check (in the case of one big end bearing only) pull off and replace the plug covers one at a time. When the cover is removed from the plug in the cylinder with the faulty big end, the knock will stop or be greatly reduced. Main bearing wear produces a heavy thumping noise when the engine is running. All cases of bearing wear result in a significant drop in oil pressure. If the oil pressure warning lamp pressure switch is removed and an oil pressure gauge temporarily screwed in, an oil pressure reading will be obtained (see 10.15, p. 150).

(7) Check the fan blades and fan belt (see (6) above). A high tension leak will cause a clicking noise. Examine the HT leads carefully and move them about when the engine is running. A leak should be detected in this way. However HT leaks are best looked for in the dark, when the engine is running. If there is any doubt about the leads, all of them should be renewed.

(8) Poor compression will result in loss of power and higher than normal fuel consumption. It may be due to the piston rings becoming gummed in their grooves or to piston ring/ cylinder bore wear. Another possible cause is badly seating valves. The cylinder head gasket may be leaking (see 1.12, p. 28).

(9) This is normally a sign of excessive piston ring/cylinder bore wear (see 1.12, p. 28).

(10) this is usually due to worn cylinder bores (see 1.12, p. 28). Excessive side clearance of the piston rings in their grooves will contribute to the trouble. Absence of any of the valve stem oil seals, one of which should be fitted below the spring retainer on each valve, will cause excessive oil consumption. Where heavy oil consumption is associated with loss of compression, it may be assumed that the cause is cylinder bore wear.

Oil leaks should not be overlooked. Such leakage is indicated by oil droppings under the car and the position of the oil on the ground often indicates the part from which it came. A common source of leakage is a defective rocker cover seal. Clean round the area of the joint with a piece of rag, and if oil is leaking, it will be seen seeping from the joint after the car has been given a short run. The remedy is to remove the cover, clean each joint face thoroughly and to fit a new seal. Tighten the cover down securely but do not over-tighten. Jointing compound may be used, but should not be necessary. When it is used it often makes it more difficult to obtain a good joint later.

(11) This is usually due to a carburettor fault, therefore see 2.2, p. 34. An engine in poor tune will use more fuel than it should, due to the cumulative effects of dirty or worn out sparking plugs with incorrectly set gaps and incorrectly set contact breaker points gap, the latter causing retarded ignition (see 4.38, p. 81).

Poor compression will tend to increase fuel consumption (see 1.12, p. 28).

(12) This may be due to a carburettor fault (see 2.2, p. 34), but it may also be due to an ignition fault (see 4.38, p. 81). The trouble may be caused by a broken valve spring or springs. Sticking valves are another possible cause of the trouble.

(13) It may be that the idling speed simply needs to be adjusted (see 2.4, p. 38). The ignition timing may be incorrect (see 4.49, p. 90). The plugs/contact breaker may need cleaning or adjustment.

(14) The idling speed may need to be adjusted or the mixture strength may be incorrect (see 2.4, p. 38). The ignition timing may be faulty (see 4.49, p. 90). Worn inlet valve guides or leaks in the intake system will cause the engine to idle fast

and make correct adjustment impossible until the faults have been found and corrected.

(15) This is due to ignition or carburettor trouble (see 2.2, p. 34, 4.38, p. 81). Plug leads may be connected in the wrong order (see Fig. 21, p. 85).

(16) Throttle linkage jammed. Rocker clearances much too great (see 1.10, p. 26).

(17) A blown cylinder head gasket will sometimes cause a squeak or whistle. Occasionally the trouble can be traced to the fan belt. Check the belt tension. If the belt shows signs of wear fit a new one. The dynamo bearings may be dry (see 4.10, p. 60). The fibre pad that runs on the contact breaker cam may be dry. Add a spot of thin oil to the cam surface.

(18) Faulty plugs will cause the trouble. Check the ignition system for loose connections or shorting leads. It is possible that the spring in the contact breaker assembly (item 11, Fig. 22, page 87) may be broken. The rocker clearance may be incorrect; the valve timing may be adrift, possibly due to an excessively worn timing chain. Excessive carbon deposit (see 1.4 below). Valves burnt or not seating correctly, sticking valves, weak or broken valve springs are other possibilities. A carburettor fault may be the cause of the trouble (see 2.2, p. 34).

(19) Severe mechanical defect, broken crankshaft or twisted connecting rod. Running the engine without oil will cause the pistons to seize.

1.4 How to Decarbonize the Engine

The burning of the fuel in the cylinders leads to a carbon deposit building up in the combustion chambers and when excessive this deposit causes pinking, loss of power and loss of engine tone generally. The remedy is to remove the cylinder head and scrape away the deposit. When is decarbonization required? The answer is that the experienced and knowledgeable driver will sense from the feel of the engine when the carbon is beginning to affect engine performance.

With modern detergent oils the carbon build up is relatively slow and most engines will run for very large mileages, even years, without need of decarbonization. On the other hand attention may be needed after a comparatively short period. However, possibly 20,000–30,000 mile intervals could be mentioned as a guide to when it may be desirable.

To decarbonize the engine it is necessary to remove and re-fit the cylinder head and this entails a fair amount of dismantling. To do it successfully the work requires a little care but many car owners carry out the work without difficulty.

First obtain a number of cardboard boxes. Make sure they have no holes in the bottom through which small parts can fall and get lost. The bits and pieces are placed in the boxes

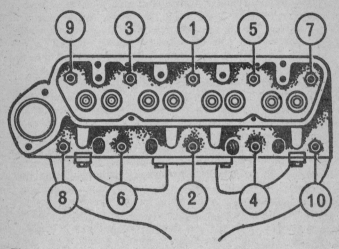

Fig. 1. The sequence in which the cylinder head bolts must be tightened. They must be tightened, a little at a time, in the numerical order shown.

as they are removed from the engine. If all the bits of one kind (those associated with the carburettor, for example) are placed in the same box, it saves the confusion that can arise if all the parts are mixed up together. It certainly speeds up re-assembly work.

Next clean the top of the engine with paraffin damped rags. When this is done dismantling work can proceed. It is, of course, assumed that you have a kit of tools (see 1.16, p. 32) and you must have in addition a valve spring compressor. Such a compressor, suitable for overhead valve engines, can be obtained at most accessory stores.

It is best to renew all gaskets and a kit containing all the gaskets required when decarbonizing can be obtained from any Ford Agent. It is usually wise (unless mileage has been minimal) to renew all the valve springs and oil seals. Have everything to hand and then proceed with the work as explained below.

(1) Disconnect the battery leads and remove the battery.

(2) Remove the radiator cap and drain the system by opening the drain taps on the right hand side of the cylinder block and the bottom of the radiator.

   If the cooling system contains anti-freeze solution you may wish to retain this for re-use.

(3) Release the air cleaner retaining screw and lift the air cleaner off the carburettor intake. Disconnect the vacuum ignition control pipe by pulling away the rubber connector, if one is fitted at this point. Alternatively detach the vacuum pipe from its connection on the inlet manifold. Disconnect the throttle and choke linkages from the carburettor. Disconnect the petrol feed pipe from the carburettor by unscrewing the union.

(4) Remove sparking plugs; number HT leads; remove HT lead from coil; then remove distributor cap and put in a safe place. Release the securing clips on each end of the top radiator hose and remove the hose. The hose will probably be adhering strongly to the stubs and will need to be pulled and twisted before it can be freed.

(5) Remove the heater hose from the cylinder head connection. Disconnect the lead from the temperature gauge sender on the front of the cylinder head. On cars fitted with an automatic choke, the choke hose must be disconnected from the inlet manifold.

(6) Detach the inlet manifold. Detach the exhaust pipe and remove the exhaust manifold.

(7) The next step is to remove the rocker shaft assembly. Remove rocker cover and gasket. Then unscrew each of the rocker shaft fixing bolts by giving a part turn commencing with an end bolt. Repeat this procedure until all the bolts are free and then remove them completely and lift the rocker shaft clear.

(8) The cylinder head is held to the cylinder block by ten bolts. The length of these bolts is not the same on all engines, high compression engines having longer bolts. On some engines the ten bolts are not all the same size

and this should be noted when removing the bolts so that they can be correctly replaced.

The bolts are unscrewed, part turn at a time, in the order shown in Fig. 1, p. 15, until free. Each bolt is then unscrewed completely and removed.

(9)   The push rods may now be lifted out. Since it is important that each rod should be replaced in the same position from which it was removed, as it is removed it should be labelled with the number of the valve which it operates, number one rod being the one nearest the radiator. Alternatively the rods may be pushed through a piece of card which is numbered to correspond to the position from which the rods were removed. If the rods are simply laid aside in their proper order they are very liable to be disturbed and mixed up accidentally.

(10) Nothing now retains the cylinder head in position except the internal deposit and the adhesion that occurs between the joint faces of the head and the joint gasket.

To break the adhesion and release the head it should be lightly tapped all round with a heavy lead hammer. An ordinary hammer may be used if a piece of hardwood is interposed between the hammer and the cylinder head. Under no circumstances should the hammer be allowed to strike the cylinder head or the head will break. If the head is very tight patience is required, but if the jarring is continued the head will eventually become free. Running the starter, if the plugs are replaced, may help free it.

(11) When the head is free it should be lifted up carefully and since it is heavy it is well to have an assistant when removing it. If it is intended to re-use the cylinder head gasket care must be taken not to damage it when the head is being removed. *Note:* If the head is difficult to remove on no account attempt to drive the end of a sharp implement such as a chisel or screwdriver into the joint to release the head. If this is done damage is liable to result.

(12) The next step is to decarbonize the piston crowns. Turn the engine by pulling on the fan belt until two of the pistons are at the top position and stuff some clean rag into the other cylinders to keep dirt out.

Scrape the carbon from the piston crowns, using a

blunt screwdriver or similar tool. Do not use a sharp tool because the pistons are made of aluminium alloy which is relatively soft and easily scratched. It is an advantage to leave a ridge of carbon round the outside edge of the pistons (close to the cylinder wall). If this is not done there will be an appreciable increase in oil consumption until the carbon builds up again at this point. If you should have an old piston ring, insert this into the cylinder and press it down into contact with the piston crown. The ring will protect the carbon where you do not want to remove it and obviates the need for care that would otherwise be necessary, but you must remember to remove the ring afterwards.

When all the carbon has been removed from the heads of these two pistons, turn the engine until the other two pistons are at the top and place clean rags in the cylinders of the first two to keep out dirt. The second two pistons are decarbonized in the same way as the first two.

(13) Attention can now be turned to the cylinder head. It is probably best to start decarbonizing it without removing the valves. An advantage of this method is that the valve seats in the head are protected from possible damage and the valves are firmly held and so can be scraped more easily, leaving less work to do to them when they are removed.

The valve heads and the combustion chambers in the head are decarbonized in the same way as the piston crowns. When this work is done the valves can be removed from the head.

(14) It is important that the valves should be replaced in the same valve guides from which they were removed. This is because parts that have been moving in contact with each other for a long time become mated and there-after work better together. Obviously this cannot apply if a new valve has to be fitted, but mated parts should not be changed unless this becomes necessary.

To make sure that the valves can be correctly re-placed, it is a good idea to take a piece of wood about a yard long and to drill eight holes in it large enough to take a valve stem. You can number the holes 1 to 8 or you can just mark the end of the wood R for radia-

18

tor. No. 1 valve is the one nearest the radiator. As the valves are removed place them in their correct holes in the wood and leave them there until they are wanted. Never have more than one valve free from the wood at a time or they will still become mixed up.

(15) To remove the valves from the cylinder head proceed thus: Sometimes the valve stems and the split taper collets become very tight in the top spring seat, tight enough to strain the spring compressor. Therefore, before using the compressor it is best to make sure any adhesion between these parts is broken. To do this obtain a piece of wood of the right size to fit into the combustion chamber so that it is about flush with the surface of cylinder head. The wood is intended to act as a support for the valve heads. With the wood in position in one of the combustion chambers and the cylinder head resting face downwards on a firm table or bench take a box spanner and hold it centrally over the valve spring seat. Strike the end of the box spanner sharply with a hammer. Since the wood support prevents the valve from opening, the spring is pushed down the valve stem and any adhesion at the collets is broken. Do this to all the valves.

Now, starting at No. 1 cylinder (the one nearest the radiator), place the forked end of the compressor on the valve spring seat. Carefully locate it centrally so that it touches the spring seat only. Place the screw end on the valve head. Tighten the screw carefully to compress the spring. Some spring compressors are adapted to fix to the cylinder head and a long lever is pulled down, an extension of which rests on the valve seat and depresses the spring. The end result is the same in either case. Make sure that the spring is compressed evenly so that there is no danger of it slipping clear of the compressor. If this happens the collets can be ejected with considerable force and may injure the operator.

When the spring is sufficiently compressed, flick the two collets out with a pocket screwdriver. Now release the compressor carefully and it will be possible to take off the valve spring, its seat and the valve seal, which is on the valve stem. It is now possible to push the valve through into the combustion chamber and to take hold of the valve head and pull it clear.

Using the same procedure, remove all the valves. If all the carbon and other deposit has not been removed from the valve heads this should now be done. All carbon should also be removed from *under* the valve heads.

Inspect each valve carefully, particularly where it seats in the cylinder head. An exhaust valve that has been leaking badly will burn. The seat of the valve may be slightly burned or part of the valve head may be burned away. In either case the valve is useless and no further attention may be paid to it. Even if not burned the valve seats may show signs of roughness—pitting and/or carbon. Valves like this may be serviceable after attention.

Carefully inspect the valve seat areas in the cylinder head. As in the case of the valves themselves, seats damaged by pitting, if it is not too bad, may be put right with the proper attention. The valve seats are rings inserted in the cylinder head and may be renewed if they become damaged or loose, in the latter case an oversize insert is required. Engines not fitted with inserted valve seats may have the port machined to take them, if this becomes necessary. But work on seats of this sort would require workshop facilities and skills which we must assume the car owner will not possess. Such work therefore is best left to a Ford Agent, since he has the required equipment and can do it efficiently. Or, in many areas, specialist engineers can be found who will undertake such work if the cylinder head is taken to their workshop.

(16) The next thing to do is to decide if new valves are necessary; burnt valves, already mentioned, obviously need to be renewed but valve stems and the guides they work in wear, and in time both need to be renewed.

Insert each valve into its own guide and, holding it open a *little*, try to rock it from side to side. There should be little or no movement. If you find that you can rock the valve, remove it from the guide and examine the stem just below the head. Worn valves will show a 'step' at this point. If excessive wear is present,

20

while a new valve will undoubtedly make things better, the only way to do the job properly is to attend to the guide also.

Valve guides are available and in some cases will be found to be fitted, but it will usually be found that the valves operate in guides integral with the cylinder head —holes drilled in the head. Where necessary these holes can be enlarged and guides fitted, but this work cannot be done by the car owner unless he has the special facilities and skill required.

(17) The next step is to grind-in the valves on their seats in the cylinder head and we will now describe how this is done.

NOTE! The inlet valves have a diffused aluminium coating at their heads which reduces wear and oxidation. Because of this *the inlet valves must not be ground-in* on their seats in the cylinder head. Valve replacement is the only remedy when inlet valves have defective seats. The inlet valve seats in the cylinder head may, however, be ground in the usual way, which is about to be described, using a *dummy* valve. The inlet valve seats in the head are 2, 3, 6, 7, numbered from the front (radiator end) of the cylinder head.

Valve grinding paste is normally obtainable in two grades, coarse and fine. Often the paste is supplied in a double ended tin, which has coarse paste in one end and fine paste in the other end.

Coarse paste is very seldom required. If the valve seats are badly pitted, the valves should be re-faced or renewed and if the trouble is in the cylinder head the seats should be skimmed with a cutter—a specialized task. Fine paste is used to clean up lightly marked seats but needs time to do it properly.

You need a valve grinding tool. This is a long wood handle with a rubber sucker fitted to one end. Make sure that the valve head is smooth and quite free from oil or grease, then moisten the sucker and press it on to the valve head.

Smear a small amount of fine grinding paste on the valve seat. The quantity of paste used should be about the size of a match head. It is a very common error to use too much paste. Insert the valve into its own guide and, holding the handle vertical, roll it between the palm of your hands, at the same time pressing downwards, so that the valve is rotated on its seat first one way and then the other. At intervals lift the valve and turn it a little while it is clear of the cylinder head seat and lower it in the new position and continue the grinding process. This lifting and part turning of the valve should be done frequently as grinding proceeds in order to obtain even grinding round the entire valve seat.

When grinding has continued for some time, remove the valve from its guide and wipe the seat free from grinding paste so that it can be examined. When the valve is properly ground there will be an unbroken, *smooth* grey area round the entire valve seat and the seat in the cylinder head. It is emphasized that the seat should be *smooth*. Even if continuous, a ridged seat is not acceptable. Grinding must be continued until a perfect seat is obtained.

When all the valves have been ground-in they should be thoroughly washed in clean paraffin and then dried with a clean cloth.

It is absolutely essential to prevent any grinding paste getting into the engine, where it will cause extremely rapid wear. Therefore, as well as making sure that the valves are free from it, clean the valve guides by pulling pieces of clean cloth moistened with paraffin through each guide, finally repeating the process with a piece of clean dry cloth. Make sure that all trace of paste has been removed from the seats and ports in the cylinder head, then wash your hands so that they are also free from grinding paste.

(18) We can now re-fit the valves into the cylinder head. Start with No. 1 valve. Lubricate the valve stem with clean engine oil, insert it in its guide and while pressing on the head to hold the stem projected fit a new valve seal to the valve stem and follow this by the valve spring. Place the spring seat on top of the spring and use the spring compressor to close the spring sufficiently to enable the two split collets to be replaced. Keep your fingers clear ; use a small screwdriver to adjust the position of the collets ; you may find a little grease helpful in holding the collets in position on the valve

22

stem. Release the spring very carefully, watching to
see that the collets remain properly located in the
spring seat and on the valve stem. If they do not then
re-compress the spring and again adjust the collects before releasing the spring. It is essential that the collets
seat properly or they will come out when the engine is
running with disastrous results.

(19) When all the valves have been re-fitted the head may be
replaced on the engine. First, remove the rags from the
cylinders and rub clean engine oil on the cylinder walls.
Turn the engine to raise and then lower the pistons in
these two cylinders. The piston rings will push up the
oil and any dirt that may have gained entry and it will
be retained by the oil at the top of the cylinders when
the pistons descend, to be wiped away with a piece of
clean cloth. Do the same with the other two cylinders,
then lubricate the walls of all the cylinders with clean
engine oil.

1.5 Re-assembly Notes

Be sure you have the correct cylinder head gasket. If you have
obtained the correct decarbonizing kit for your model, the
gasket will be correct.

Ensure that the cylinder block joint face is clean and place
the gasket on the block with the side marked 'TOP' upper-
most. Jointing compound should not normally be required. A
difficulty arises in correctly locating the gasket. Fitting tools
are available, but are not likely to be in the possession of the
car owner. One way to do it is to obtain two cylinder head
bolts and saw the heads off. If, after the gasket is placed in
position, the headless bolts are screwed into diagonally opposite
site corners they will locate the gasket and act as a guide to
the cylinder head. The headless bolts must only be partly
screwed into the block so as to leave projecting ends after the
cylinder head has been fitted and thus allow their removal
with a pair of pliers.

The only alternative to this scheme is to use stiff grease to
hold the gasket on the block. Two cylinder head bolts are
then fitted to diagonally opposite holes in the cylinder head
and the head is very carefully lowered, engaging the bolts in
their holes before the cylinder head is fully lowered. Care
must be taken not to damage the gasket. The cylinder head

joint face must be clean. Cylinder head joint leakage is often due to dirt trapped in the joint.

With the head in position and the gasket properly located, fit all the cylinder head securing bolts and screw up finger tight. Note that there may be two bolts shorter than the others.

Using a ring spanner tighten all the bolts progressively, a little at a time, in the numerical sequence shown in Fig. 1. Final tightening should be done with a torque spanner. The torque ratings of these bolts are given in 10.8, p. 148.

Replace the push rods in the same positions from which they were removed. Make sure that all the rods are fully down and thus located in their respective tappets.

Re-fit the rocker shaft assembly, carefully ensuring that the ball ends of the adjusting screws on the rockers engage properly with the cups in the ends of the push rods. Screw in all the securing bolts finger tight, then run along all the bolts with a ring spanner tightening each bolt a little at a time.

The next step is to adjust the rocker clearances (see 1.10, p. 26). Re-fit the rocker cover joint gasket (a new gasket should be used), the rocker cover and its securing screws.

With the valve clearances adjusted the radiator hose can be re-connected and all the other parts re-assembled. Do not overtighten the cover securing screws. Re-fill the cooling system after all drain taps/plugs are closed, including anti-freeze if required. Inspect the system for leaks, start the engine and again check for leaks. After the first fifty miles check the cylinder head nuts for tightness, and tighten to correct torque, if necessary.

1.6 Pistons and Cylinder Bores

After machining operations are completed the size of each bore is stamped on the top face of the block or on the right hand side of the block near the top face. Pistons are similarly size graded to facilitate selective assembly, so that fine clearances can be maintained. The grade marking is stamped on the piston crown.

The piston pin is offset towards the thrust side of the engine (left hand side) by .04 in. (1.0 m.m.). Pistons must be fitted so that the arrow on the piston head points towards the front of the engine.

Cylinder liners of different outside diameters are available.

Worn cylinders are reconditioned by machining the bores to suitable limits to accept a liner which is then pressed into position and machined to give a suitable piston/bore clearance for the pistons used.

1.7 Oil Filter

The oil filter on all engines is a full flow unit. The filter element must be renewed at intervals, see chap 9. To renew a filter element, unscrew the bottom securing screw, this is a long bolt which passes up into the filter head. Remove the bolt and withdraw the filter bowl. Be prepared for some oil spillage when the bowl is removed. With the bowl removed remove the filter element and dispose of it. Clean the bowl in paraffin and dry. Fit a new sealing ring to the filter head. Do not fit the ring in the groove at one point and then run the finger round on top of the ring. This is likely to stretch it and end in a loop which will be trapped across the joint when the bowl is fitted. Press the ring into the groove at four equidistant points, then press in all round. Fit the element and bowl and secure with the long bolt, after fitting a new washer to the bolt head. Do not overtighten (see 10.8, p. 148). Start the engine and check the filter for leakage.

1.8 Engine Oil Level

A dipstick is situated at the left hand side of the engine. To check the sump oil level, withdraw the dipstick and wipe it free from oil on a piece of clean cloth; then fully insert the dipstick and withdraw it. The oil level will be indicated by the oil wetted portion of the dipstick. Maintain the oil level up to the 'full' mark by adding approved oil (see 10.18, p. 150). The engine may be safely run if the oil level is between the 'danger' and 'full' marks but not if it is in the area of the dipstick marked 'danger'.

Add oil, as required, after removing the filler cap on the rocker cover.

The oil level should be checked with the car on level ground and with the engine stopped. Make sure the dipstick is pressed fully down when taking an oil level reading.

1.9 Draining the Oil

The oil should be drained from the engine sump and new oil added at the recommended intervals. See Chapter 9. For the sump capacity see 10.5, p. 144. The oil should be drained when hot. Unscrew and remove the drain plug from the bottom of the engine sump on the right hand side. Allow about 15 minutes for the engine to drain. If the car is a second hand one and there is doubt about proper maintenance having been carried out, it would be wise to flush the engine out. To do this re-fit the drain plug as soon as the sump is drained and fill with flushing oil up to the full mark on the dipstick. Run the engine at tick-over speed for a few minutes, then drain out the flushing oil. Re-fit the drain plug and fill up with approved engine oil. Change the oil filter element as described in 1.7 above.

1.10 Rocker Clearance Adjustment

The rocker clearances are adjusted as explained below. For the correct clearances refer to 10.17, p. 150.

To ensure that the valve operated by the rocker being adjusted is closed (which is essential), adjust the rockers in the sequence shown below:

With these valves open	Adjust these valves
1 and 6	3 and 8
2 and 4	5 and 7
3 and 8	1 and 6
5 and 7	2 and 4

Method of Adjustment:

If the rocker adjuster is fitted with a locknut adjust the clearances this way: place a ring spanner on the adjuster locknut and release the nut. While still holding the spanner in position on the nut, turn the adjuster with a screwdriver until a feeler gauge of the correct thickness will just enter the gap between rocker and valve stem. There must be no up-and-down play but no force should be required to slide the blade into the gap. The blade should move freely in the gap with slight drag. When the correct adjustment has been obtained tighten the locknut while holding the adjuster with the screwdriver to maintain the adjustment. Re-check the adjustment when the locknut is tight. Adjust all the rockers in this way.

If the adjusters on the rocker arms do not have locknuts, as is the case on some Escorts, (see Fig 2), the adjustment is obtained simply by turning the adjuster as required with a ring spanner, and using a feeler gauge to check the clearance as already described. These adjusters are self locking and once set to the correct adjustment will maintain it.

Fig. 2 Adjusting rocker/valve clearance. A feeler gauge is used to set the clearance between the rocker and the valve. This shows the self locking type of adjuster. The other type of adjuster has a locknut.

1.11 Valve Timing

With the sparking plugs removed, turn the engine so that No. 1 piston (the one nearest the radiator) is at TDC (top dead centre) on the compression stroke. The compression stroke can be found by lightly closing the plug hole in No. 1 cylinder with the thumb, while the engine is turned slowly. Pressure will be felt (air escaping past the thumb) when the piston is rising on the compression stroke.

With the piston known to be rising on the compression stroke, the timing marks of the two chain wheels can be aligned. The marks must be in line when the wheels are turned and so that the marks are close together. The timing chain can then be fitted, making sure the chain wheels do not move. Check when the chain is fitted that the two timing marks still align.

1.12 Loss of Compression

Loss of compression means loss of power and increased fuel consumption. It may be due simply to excessive piston ring and bore wear in which case the remedy is to have the cylinder bores linered and new pistons and rings fitted. However the trouble may be caused by broken piston rings or, more likely, piston rings stuck in their grooves. The fault may occur in one or more cylinders.

A blown cylinder head gasket can cause loss of compression but will usually produce other symptoms such as water in the oil and, conversely, oil in the cooling water. There may be an escape of gas to the outside of the cylinder, it depends on how the gasket fails. Escape of gas to the atmosphere may cause a whistling sound. Passing the hand round the cylinder head joint when the engine is running will reveal such a fault. MIND THE FAN! Obviously a loose or cracked cylinder head would have the same effect as a faulty gasket.

A common cause of poor compression is leaky valves, resulting from normal wear and tear, but valve rocker clearances too tightly adjusted will cause the trouble. If the engine has been run for any length of time with the rocker adjustment too tight, correct adjustment will not then cure the trouble and it will be necessary to remove the cylinder head and to renew or grind-in the valves (see 1.4, p. 14).

To check the engine cylinders for compression, securely chock the front wheels, jack up one of the rear wheels clear of the ground and engage top gear. The ignition and handbrake must be 'off'. Remove all the sparking plugs but one. Turn the engine by rotating the rear wheel. Considerable resistance should be felt as the piston goes over compression. Remove the plug and screw in the plug of another cylinder and again turn the piston over compression by means of the rear wheel. Repeat the process with each cylinder. The compression in each cylinder should feel about the same.

To find if poor compression in a cylinder is due to piston ring or valve leakage, remove the plug and pour about a table spoonful of clean engine oil into the cylinder, replace the plug and check the compression in the way already explained. If the compression in the weak cylinder is not improved it is the valves that are at fault. If compression is improved, the piston rings are not providing a good seal.

1.13 The Lubrication System

The engine oil is contained in the sump, from whence it is drawn through a spring loaded filter gauze by the oil pump which is mounted externally on the right hand side of the cylinder block. Two types of interchangeable pumps are used, a vane type and a bi-rotor type. Oil from the pump passes through the full flow oil filter, which is bolted to the pump body, into the gallery which is a drillway in the cylinder block. From the gallery oil is pressure fed to the main bearings, big end bearings and camshaft bearings. The cylinder walls are lubricated partly by splash and partly by oil jets from the big end bearings.

The timing chain is lubricated by an oil jet and a reduced pressure feed is provided for the valve rockers via a drillway in the rocker shaft. The oil pump is provided with a non-adjustable plunger type relief valve. The oil, after passing through the various lubrication points drains to the sump, the oil from the rocker shaft draining down the push rod tubes to lubricate the cams and tappets. After returning to the sump the oil is re-circulated through the system.

1.14 Fault Symptoms

(1) Oil consumption too high
(2) Oil pressure warning light does not go out when the engine is running, or the pressure gauge shows an unusually low reading.
(3) Oil pressure too low.
(4) Oil pressure too high.
(5) Oil level in sump increases though no oil is added.
(6) Blue smoke in large quantities is emitted from the exhaust.

1.15 Causes and Cures

(1) This may be due to cylinder bore/piston ring wear but this would only be likely in an engine that had seen much service. When such a fault is present much blue smoke is emitted from the exhaust. A similar effect occurs if the piston rings become stuck in their grooves.

The fault may be due to worn valve guides, faulty valve stem oil seals or to the absence of these seals. A common cause of heavy oil consumption is leakage. Such leakage will be evident by oil marks under the car when it has been standing for some time. The position of the marks on the ground will give a good indication of where leakage is taking place. If the engine is thoroughly cleaned and then inspected after a 5–6 mile run, any leakage should be seen. A poor fit at the rocker cover joint will result in the loss of considerable quantities of oil. Make sure this joint is sound. Make sure that both joint faces are clean; lumps of old jointing compound will spoil the joint. The joint gasket must be sound; if there is any doubt about this a new gasket should be fitted.

(2) If this happens immediately stop the engine and check the sump level (see 1.8, p. 25). If the oil level is normal it must be assumed that there is a fault in the lubrication system, and the engine must not be run until the fault is found and remedied. It may be that the fault lies in the oil pressure warning light circuit or switch. The switch is located adjacent to the oil pump on the right hand side of the engine. Detach the wire from the switch. If the light remains on there is a short circuit in the wire to earth at some point. This test is made with the ignition switched *on*. To prove if the switch is at fault it is necessary to substitute a new one. Alternatively, unscrew the switch and screw in an oil pressure gauge. It will then be possible to visually observe the oil pressure in the system when the engine is running. For correct pressure see 10.15, p. 150. If the pressure registered on the gauge is correct, the switch is faulty and a new one is required. More causes are given in (3) below.

If the oil warning light comes on when driving in a situation where assistance is difficult to obtain, remove the rocker cover, start the engine and let it run no faster than tick-over speed. Note if oil is oozing from the rockers as it normally does; if this *is* the case it is probably safe to drive slowly to a point where assistance can be obtained.

(3) Low oil pressure is indicated by the oil warning light remaining on when the engine is running, see (2) above, or by the gauge. Suspected low oil pressure if a warning light only is fitted should be checked by removing the oil pressure switch and screwing in an oil pressure gauge. For the correct oil pressure see 10.15, p. 150. Low oil pressure may be due to low oil level in the sump (see 1.8, p. 25), or to worn big end or main bearings. It is possible after long service that the pump

intake has become clogged with sludge. An air leak in the suction side of the pump or a faulty pump will cause low oil pressure. The use of incorrect oil (viscosity too low) will result in low oil pressure as will oil thinned by dilution with fuel, due to incorrect use of the choke. It is possible that the relief valve may be stuck open or the spring may have become weak.

(4) This is unlikely to occur. The fault could be due to the use of unsuitable oil (viscosity too high), to an obstruction in the

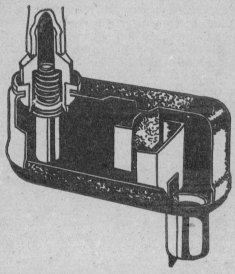

Fig. 3. Crankcase emission valve. This is used to ventilate the crankcase. It is not fitted to all models. Some Escorts have crankcase ventilation via a vent opening and gauze in the oil filler cap.

system or to fitting an unsuitable spring in the pressure relief valve.

(5) This would indicate that there is a water leak from the cooling system.

(6) This is normally the symptom of a worn engine (cylinder bore and piston ring wear). It could be due to the piston rings being stuck in their grooves.

1.16 Tools

The reader mechanically inclined will probably have a good selection of spanners, screwdrivers, pliers, etc.

Suitable sets of American spanners can be obtained at motor accessory and tool stores. Ideally, both open ended and ring spanners should be available, the ring spanners being particularly useful (sometimes essential) when tight nuts and/or bolts are encountered.

1.17 Emission Valve

It is necessary to clean the emission control valve at intervals and to do this it is necessary to remove the valve from its location in the rear of the carburettor. The purpose of the valve is to control the volume of air flow through the crankcase ventilation system, increasing and decreasing the flow in proportion to the load on the engine.

To gain access to the valve first remove the connecting hose. The valve assembly is plugged into a rubber bush and may be pulled clear. When removed extract the internal circlip using a pair of circlip pliers; the valve seal, valve and spring may then be removed in that order. Wash the parts in a small quantity of petrol and reassemble. Plug the valve into its former position and re-connect the hose. Fig. 3 shows details of the emission valve.

2
The Fuel System

2.1 General

The fuel tank is located below the floor of the luggage compartment (rear floor in the Estate car). The engine mounted mechanical fuel pump draws fuel from the tank and delivers it to the carburettor via a fuel line composed of nylon tubing.

A float operated rheostat, mounted inside the petrol tank works the fuel gauge. The gauge gives its reading according to the variation in the output voltage of the rheostat. A voltage stabiliser ensures that this reading is not affected by variations in battery voltage (due to load demands) state of charge of the battery (within wide limits) or generator voltage.

On some Escorts an automatic choke is fitted. The choke is operated by the expansion and contraction of a bi-metallic coil contained in a watertight compartment on the carburettor, through which water from the cooling system flows.

GT engined Escorts are fitted with a dual barrel Weber carburettor, see Fig. 4. In this carburettor the functions of the single barrel carburettor are divided between the two barrels. The throttle valve in each barrel opening in a sequential relationship. The primary barrel throttle opens first and the secondary barrel throttle afterwards but both throttle valves reach the fully open position at the same time.

The starting, idling and accelerator pump systems are located in the primary barrel. The main progression system is common to both barrels, but the secondary barrel system is fully operational only when the engine is on full throttle.

The types of carburettors fitted to different models are listed below. See Figs. 4 and 5.

1100 c.c Engines
Ford single barrel with accelerator pump and semi-auto-

33

B

matic choke. Type: C7AH-A, or with emission reduction (crankcase emission valve fitted), C7AH-E.

1300 c.c. Engines (not GT).

Ford single barrel with accelerator pump and fully or semi-automatic choke. Types: Semi-automatic choke C7AH-B. Automatic choke C7AH-D.

GT Engines.

Weber double barrel. Type: DGF-HA.

The reader is strongly advised not to dismantle the carburettor, except in so far as this may become necessary to clean the float chamber or jets.

2.2 Fault Symptoms

(1) Starting is difficult.
(2) The engine will not idle, stalls easily.
(3) The engine lacks power.
(4) Engine spits back—spitting and banging in air cleaner.
(5) Engine hunts—idling speed uneven.
(6) Petrol runs or drips from carburettor.
(7) Mixture strength too weak.
(8) Mixture strength too rich.
(9) Fuel consumption excessive.
(10) Acceleration poor.
(11) Engine runs erratically.
(12) Engine overheats.
(13) Pump faulty—delivers no fuel or insufficient fuel.

2.3 Causes and Cures

(1) This may be an ignition fault, therefore see 4.38, p. 81. If the mixture is too rich the engine will be very difficult to start. The usual cause of this is faulty choke operation or excessive use of the choke. The choke must not be used when starting a warm engine. The remedy is to open the throttle wide (accelerator pedal fully down) and to operate the starter. Reduce the throttle as required when the engine starts.

The engine cannot start if no fuel is reaching the carburettor. Check that there is fuel in the tank. Occasionally the fuel gauge develops a fault and registers some fuel when in fact the tank is empty. Check that the (manual) choke is operating correctly. If the operating wire is adjusted too short, movement of the engine on its mountings may operate the

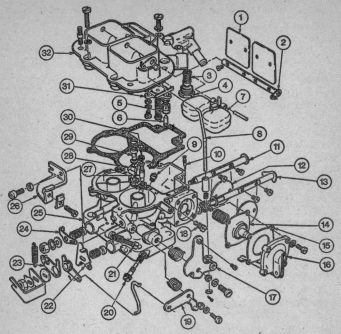

Fig 4. Showing all the parts of the Weber Twin barrel
Carburettor.

Key: 1. Choke plate; 2. Choke plate shaft; 3. Filter; 4. Filter
retaining screw; 5. Needle valve housing; 6. Needle valve; 7.
Float; 8. Choke operating link; 9. Main jet (primary); 10. Accelerator blanking plug; 11. Secondary throttle shaft; 12. Throttle
plate; 13. Primary throttle shaft; 14. Accelerator pump diaphragm; 15. Gasket; 16. Accelerator pump cover; 17. Fast idle
cam; 18. Slow running jet and holder assembly; 19. Choke lever;
20. Volume control screw; 21. Fast idle screw; 22. Throttle stop
lever; 23. Throttle control lever; 24. Secondary throttle lever; 25.
Lower body; 26. Choke cable retainer plate; 27. Primary diffuser
tube; 28. Accelerator pump discharge jet; 29. Accelerator pump
discharge ball check valve; 30. Primary main air correction jet;
31. Spring loaded diaphragm assembly; 32. Upper body.

choke control slightly. The remedy is to have a little play in
the choke wire. Make sure that the choke is moving completely to the 'Off' position when the knob is pushed in.

If the float needle sticks it will prevent fuel entering the carburettor but this fault is indicated only if the fuel pump is proved to be functioning correctly.

Dirt and/or water in the petrol will cause difficult starting. Make sure the fuel filter is clean; if necessary clean out the carburettor float chamber and at the same time check that there is no dirt on the float needle seat; in some cases this will cause the needle to stick. If any appreciable quantity of water should accumulate in the fuel tank, it will probably be necessary to remove and drain the tank to get rid of the water. Check that the fuel tank vent pipe is free of blockage (the vent pipe free end passes through the luggage boot floor via a rubber grommet). If air cannot enter the tank the pump cannot draw fuel from it. Check that the throttle linkage is operating the butterfly throttle(s) properly. The throttle cable may be stiff or stuck in its outer casing.

(2) This may simply be incorrect adjustment of the throttle stop. If it is, turning the screw in slightly will cure the trouble. This assumes that the mixture strength is correctly adjusted (see 2.4, p. 38).

(3) Too rich or too weak a mixture will affect the power output. A clogged air cleaner will result in a rich mixture while a leakage at the inlet manifold and carburettor attachment joints will allow air to be drawn in, making the mixture too weak. The trouble may be an ignition fault, (see 4.38, p. 81). The engine may need to be decarbonised or may be excessively worn. Binding brakes will result in apparent loss of power (see 7.4, p. 116 and 7.7, p. 117). It is possible that the fuel pump is delivering insufficient fuel, therefore see 2.6, p. 41.

(4) This may be due to an ignition fault (see 4.38, p. 81), or it may be caused by weak mixture, see 2.4 below. There may be water in the fuel system. Burnt exhaust valves can cause the trouble as can running without an air cleaner. Leakage at the carburettor and inlet manifold attachment joints will result in weak mixture due to air being drawn into the system.

(5) This may be an ignition fault, therefore see 4.38, p. 81. When due to the carburettor it is a mixture strength fault, or the idling speed may simply need to be properly adjusted (see 2.4 below).

(6) This is commonly due to grit or other dirt on the float needle seat which prevents the needle shutting off the petrol

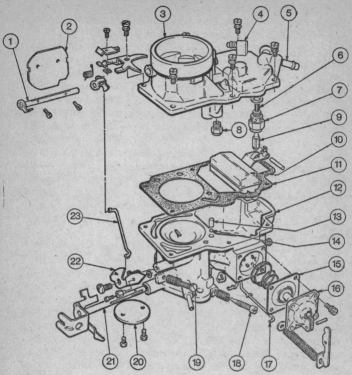

Fig. 5. Showing all the parts of the Ford Carburettor.

Key: 1. Choke plate shaft; 2. Choke plate; 3. Upper body; 4. External vent; 5. Fuel inlet; 6. Filter; 7. Needle valve housing; 8. Main jet; 9. Needle valve; 10. Float; 11. Gasket; 12. Lower body; 13. Weight; 14. Ball; 15. Accelerator pump diaphragm; 16. Accelerator pump cover; 17. Accelerator pump rod; 18. Volume control screw; 19. Throttle stop screw; 20. Throttle plate; 21. Throttle shaft; 22. Fast idle cam; 23. Choke operating link.

supply from the pump when the fuel in the float chamber reaches its proper level. If this happens the pump will continue to operate and flooding will take place. The remedy is to thoroughly clean out the float chamber and to wash the float needle and its seat in petrol. The fuel system filters should also be cleaned. It may be necessary in an extreme case to clean the fuel lines to and from the tank and the tank itself. Punctured floats are now very rare, but it is worth checking by shaking the float, while it is held close to the ear, that there is no fuel in it. A faulty float must be renewed. The fuel level in the float chamber may be too high and require adjustment. Excessive engine vibration, due to loose or faulty engine mountings can cause flooding.

(7) This may be due to leakage in the induction system joints (inlet manifold and carburettor). The carburettor adjustment may be incorrect, see 2.4 below. The fuel pump may be faulty (see 2.6, p. 41).

(8) Check that the air cleaner is not choked and that the carburettor is not flooding (fuel dripping from carburettor). The carburettor adjustment may be incorrect, see 2.4 below.

(9) As for (8) above.

(10) This may be an ignition fault see 4.38, p. 81. If due to the carburettor it is probably caused by incorrect adjustment (see 2.4 below).

(11) This may be due to incorrect adjustment of the carburettor. A choked air cleaner will cause the engine to hunt or to run unevenly. An air leakage in the induction system will result in high engine RPM (revs) when the engine should be idling which cannot be adjusted down.

(12) This may be an ignition fault (see 4.38, p. 81) or may be due to a weak mixture. It is possible that the fuel pump is faulty or there may be an air leakage on the suction side of the pump. There may be a blockage in the lines or in the fuel tank. Check that the tank air vent pipe is clear.

(13) This may be due to a fault in the pump (see 2.6, p. 41) or to air leakage in the line from the pump to the tank. There may be a blockage in the fuel lines or in the tank outlet. Check that the vent pipe is clear.

2.4 Slow Running Adjustment

Before commencing to adjust the slow running refer to 1.10, p. 26 and make sure the rocker clearances are correctly set. Make sure the contact breaker points gap is correctly set (see 4.45, p. 89). Have the engine at normal operating temperature. The air cleaner should be serviced to ensure that it is having no choking effect on the engine. Two adjustments are provided. Refer to Fig. 6.

(1) The slow running adjustment screw or throttle stop.

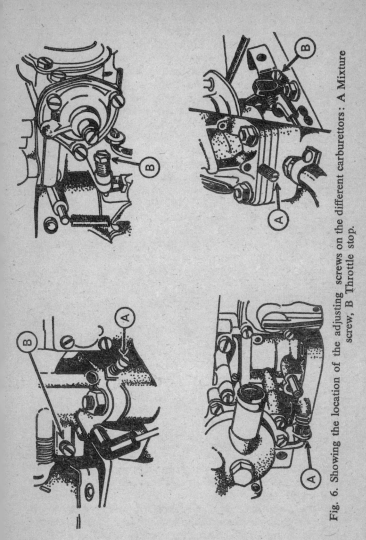

Fig. 6. Showing the location of the adjusting screws on the different carburettors: A Mixture screw, B Throttle stop.

This adjusts the engine slow running speed by providing a pre-set throttle position. This is screw B (top right) in Fig. 6, Ford carburettor, and screw B (bottom right) Weber carburettor.

(2) The volume control screw. This varies the petrol/air mixture drawn into the engine when it is idling. This is screw A Ford carburettor (top left) and screw A Weber (bottom right).

To adjust the idling speed first screw in the throttle stop screw B until the engine is idling too fast. Now slowly unscrew the volume control screw A to enrich the mixture until the engine commences to 'Hunt' or run unevenly, then slowly turn the screw in again (clockwise) until the engine runs evenly. Now screw out the throttle stop B slowly to reduce the idling speed until it is correct. If the engine idling speed becomes uncertain (may stall) very slightly turn in screw A. Repeat this procedure until the engine runs evenly at a satisfactory idling speed. Do not attempt to obtain too low an idling speed; a gentle tick-over cannot be expected on the modern high compression engine.

2.5 Accelerator Pump Adjustment

The pump is of the diaphragm type, located in a squared shape housing on the side of both Ford and Weber carburettors. The diaphragm is connected by a rod and spring to the throttle valve, the rod being free on the pump operating level. If the accelerator is quickly depressed the spring is compressed and moves the pump level to cause a small quantity of fuel to be injected through a metering jet into the intake. Suitably disposed ball valves maintain the correct direction of fuel flow and provide a seal against the entry of air. The stroke of the pump is adjusted by expanding or closing the U bend in the rod which passes through the operating spring. The correct procedure for adjusting the pump is explained below.

(1) The air cleaner must be removed.

(2) Completely close the throttle valve (butterfly valve) by unscrewing the throttle stop (B) Fig. 6. Fully press in the pump operating plunger in the centre of the housing and measure the gap between the plunger and its operating lever. The correct clearance is: For 1100 c.c. engines and manual choke: 0·105–0·115" (2·67–2·92

mm) or if fitted with an automatic choke: 0·120–0·130″ (3·05–3·30 mm). For all 1300 engines the clearance is 0·145–0·155″ (3·68–3·93 mm).

2.6 To Test the Fuel Pump

Disconnect the pipe from the pump to the carburettor at the carburettor end. Tie a plastic bag on the pipe so that the end of the pipe is inside the bag. This is to prevent petrol being ejected over the engine. Petrol is dangerous! There must be NO flame or fire within 20 yards (19 m) when petrol is exposed to the air. Run the engine on the starter. The pump should copiously eject petrol into the bag. It should be obvious from the quantity of petrol pumped into the bag by the pump whether the pump is working satisfactorily or not.

It is an advantage if the end of the pipe can be placed in a clear container partly filled with fuel so that it is submerged. It will then be possible to observe if any air bubbles appear, indicating that air is being carried in the fuel and therefore that an air leakage is present somewhere in the suction line to the pump. Make sure, however, that there is sufficient fuel in the tank.

If the pump works satisfactorily during the above test, the only fault that can stop fuel entering the carburettor is a stuck float needle. If the pump fails to deliver sufficient fuel it may be because it is drawing in air somewhere in the line from the tank to the pump, therefore check this line carefully. The pump may be removed from the engine and tested by hand. If a short length of pipe is connected to the pump inlet and the free end of this pipe is immersed in a small container of fuel it should work if operated by hand. The pump may be operated by forcing the rocker up and releasing it. Do this several times.

The usual causes of pump failure are a punctured diaphragm or a sticking valve, this last fault probably being caused by dirt on the valve seat. If the pump is very old the operating linkage may be worn, the only remedy being to fit a new pump. It may be that the flange screws are slack thus allowing the pump to draw in air. Another possible cause of failure is an air leakage at the base of the clear bowl, due to a faulty sealing washer or to the bowl not being securely tightened down. It is assumed, of course, that the filters are not blocked since this would clearly obstruct the passage of the fuel.

A faulty pump, if it is of any age, is best replaced with an exchange unit, but repair kits are available and it is not a difficult matter to dismantle and re-assemble the pump.

2.7 Cleaning the Fuel Pump Filter

Unscrew the bowl retaining nut and move the wire stirrup sideways, clear of bowl. Pull off and clean the filter gauze using a small quantity of petrol and a soft brush. Remove sediment from the cavity in the pump body. Replace filter gauze and bowl. The bowl sealing gasket must be sound or the pump will not operate. Reposition stirrup and tighten bowl securing nut.

2.8 Fuel Pump Repair

The pump may be removed from the engine by disconnecting the fuel pipes and releasing the pump fixings. To dismantle the pump, proceed as explained below. See Fig. 7.

(1) Release the stirrup screw and remove the clear bowl. Remove the gasket at the base of the bowl and the gauze filter.

(2) Make a line across the flange joint. Do this with a small hacksaw or a sharp instrument (not a pencil: pencil marks rub out). Make the mark near the diaphragm tab (smaller tab, if two are present). Remove the screws and washers round the flange joint. The top part of the pump body may now be lifted clear.

(3) To release the diaphragm from the rocker arm link in the bottom part of the pump body give it a quarter turn in either direction and pull away. Now remove the diaphragm spring, oil seal and washer.

(4) The valves may be removed for replacement by relieving the staking holding them in position. The new valves must be placed in position and re-staked at a new point. On some pumps the valves are held in position by a plate which is fixed by two screws. Removal of the screws enables the plate and valves to be removed.

Re-assembly Notes: The pump is assembled by reversing the dismantling procedure. When fitting the diaphragm, engage the end of the rod in the slot in the end of the link and give a quarter turn to connect the rod to the link, but the pump must

Fig. 7. Fuel pump.

be assembled so that the alignment marks on the two parts of the body coincide and in addition the smaller tab must be located in the same relationship to the mating mark as it was before the pump was dismantled. The screws should be screwed up only lightly at first and the pump operated several times to centralize the diaphragm. The screws are then fully tightened.

If difficulty is experienced in re-fitting the pump to the engine, this will be because the operating cam is in the 'Lift' position. If the starter is 'Flicked' to turn the engine by a small amount, the pump should then fit.

2.9 Air Filter Element Renewal (Ford Carburettor)

Unscrew the centre bolt retaining the filter top in position and remove the top. On later models the top is held in position by four retaining screws and these must be removed before the top can be lifted off. With the top removed the element can be lifted out. Two types of element are used, paper and oil wetted gauze. The paper type should be shaken clear of all dust and examined for damage. The slightest damage renders it unfit for further use and a new one must be fitted; otherwise it may be put back unless due for replacement (see Chapter 9). The oil wetted gauze filter element should be removed and washed thoroughly in petrol and allowed to dry. The element is then thoroughly wetted with engine oil and refitted. Then fit and secure the top cover.

2.10 Air Filter Element Renewal (Weber Carburettor)

Unscrew the two cover retaining nuts and remove the cover. The paper element may now be lifted out. Shake the element clear of all dust and examine carefully for damage. Renew the element if the slightest damage is found or if it is due for replacement (see Chapter 9). Otherwise re-fit the element in the filter body and re-fit and secure the top cover.

2.11 To Remove the Air Filter

Proceed as described in 2.9 or 2.10, depending on the type of carburettor fitted. With the top cover and filter element removed the Ford carburettor air filter may be lifted off the carburettor. In the case of the Weber carburettor, after the top cover and filter has been removed, release the nut locking tabs by bending them back and remove the nuts. Remove the

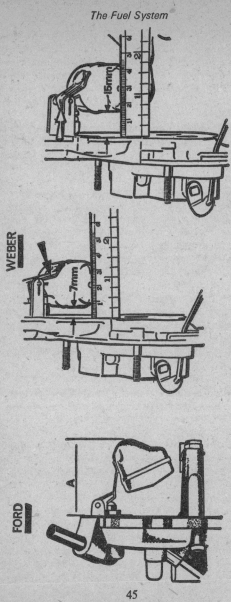

Fig. 8. Float level adjustment. The float level adjustment is important because it determines the petrol level in the float chamber in relation to the jets.

locking tab plates, plain and rubber washers and lift the air filter clear of the carburettor.

The air filter is re-fitted by reversing the removal procedure. When replacing the filter top cover align the arrow on the cover with the spout.

2.12 Float Level Setting (Ford Carburettor)

(1) Remove the air filter, see 2.11.

(2) Disconnect the fuel pipe and vent pipe from the carburettor top.

(3) Take out the screws attaching the carburettor top to the body. Ensure that the joint gasket comes away with the carburettor top. Un-hook the choke wire as the top is lifted.

(4) Hold the carburettor top vertical (see Fig. 8). Measure the distance A with the joint gasket in position. This distance should be 1·12 to 1·14 in. (28·5 to 28·9 mm). If necessary bend the tab resting against the needle valve to obtain the correct measurement.

(5) Hold the carburettor top horizontal (normal position when on carburettor). Re-measure distance A, with joint gasket in position. The distance should be increased to 1·38 to 1·40 in. (35·1 to 35·5 mm). If this measurement is not obtained bend the second tab (on the float hinge, acting as a stop) until the correct measurement is obtained.

(6) Re-fit the top (with gasket) to the carburettor. Position the choke cable bracket below the rear left hand top retaining screw. Tighten all the screws while holding the choke lever in the closed position.

Re-assembly Notes: When fitting the carburettor top be sure to hook up the choke operating link wire so that the lever system works correctly. Check this while the carburettor top is held in position, before tightening the retaining screws. If the choke is found to be inoperative, remove the top again so that the choke operating lever can be properly positioned. Do not force the lever to its proper position with the top screwed down, or damage is likely to occur.

When the top is off the carburettor, the accelerator pump discharge valve is exposed and there is danger that the valve and weight may be inadvertently ejected if the throttle linkage is operated. Take care that this does not happen, as these parts could fall through the carburettor into the engine.

2.13 Float Level Setting (Weber Carburettor)

(1) Remove the air cleaner.

(2) Disconnect the fuel pipe, and choke plate operating rod at lower end.

(3) Remove the carburettor top retaining screws and lift the top off the body. Ensure the gasket comes away with the top.

(4) Hold the carburettor top so that it is vertical (quarter turn from its normal position) with the float hanging down, see Fig. 8.

(5) With the gasket in position on the carburettor top, press the float very lightly towards the carburettor top and measure the distance between it and the gasket as shown by dark arrow. This distance should be 7 mm; if it is not adjust by bending the arm between the pivot and the float, at the float end. With the measurement correct at 7 mm the tab, which is hooked to the needle valve should be in light contact with the ball and vertical.

(6) Now lightly press the float to the limit of its travel in the opposite direction (away from the float chamber top) as shown by white arrow. The measurement should be 15 mm. Adjust, if necessary to obtain this measurement by bending the tab which abuts the needle valve housing.

(7) Re-fit gasket to carburettor followed by top. Re-fit choke plate operating rod.

(8) Re-connect the fuel pipe and fit air filter, as described in 2.11 above.

3

The Cooling System

3.1 General

Water is circulated through the cylinder jacket and radiator by a pump, belt driven from the engine crankshaft. In its passage through the water jacket the water absorbs heat from the cylinders and cylinder head, this heat being subsequently removed from the water during its passage through the radiator, due to the flow of air through the radiator matrix. Air flow through the radiator is assisted by a fan attached to the water pump. A thermostat in the system restricts the flow of water through the radiator when the engine is warming up and thus prevents over cooling during this period.

3.2 Fault Symptoms

(1) The engine overheats.
(2) The engine runs too cool.
(3) The radiator needs frequent topping up.
(4) There is oil in the cooling water.

3.3 Causes and Cures

(1) The overheating may not be due to a fault in the cooling system. It may be due to an ignition fault (see 4.38, p. 81) or to a carburettor fault (see 2.2, p. 34). If overheating occurs suddenly, check at once that the ignition warning light is out when the engine is running. If not, the fan belt is broken or slack and this is the cause.

Shortage of oil in the engine will cause overheating. Low water level in the radiator will cause overheating, as will a restriction in the water circulation. Such restriction may be a deposit of lime in the radiator or a faulty thermostat (see 3.6, p. 52). Occasionally connecting hoses will become obstructed and need replacement. The radiator exterior may have become partially blocked with mud or insects. Clear it by directing a water jet on the radiator so that the water passes from rear to front meanwhile protecting the engine from splash with a sheet of plastic.

(2) Overcooling is only likely to occur in very cold weather and will be shown by the temperature gauge. An over cooled engine will use more fuel than it should. If the trouble should arise the remedy is to blank off a small part of the radiator with a piece of card, but care is needed or the result will be overheating, and continued overheating will inevitably bring serious results.

A faulty thermostat, one that stays open all the time will result in an engine that heats up slowly when it is started from cold (see 3.6, p. 52). A faulty temperature gauge or sender may result in a 'Cold' reading although the engine is at normal operating temperature.

(3) This may be a leak in the radiator or in the connecting hoses or their joints. Leakage may sometimes be pinpointed via water on the ground when the car has been standing for some time.

A cracked cylinder block, or more likely, a faulty cylinder head gasket may allow water to enter the sump. This will cause the level in the sump to rise, and the dipstick will give evidence of the presence of water.

If the leakage is slight there may not be more than a film of oil on the top of the water in the radiator. Leakage of this kind may be due to slack cylinder head bolts or to a distorted cylinder head. A distorted head may be trued by an engineer with a surface grinder or linisher. In order to avoid distortion in the cylinder head it is most important to tighten the bolts gradually and in the proper sequence as shown by Fig. 1. This applies also when the bolts are released when the cylinder head is removed.

(4) The presence of oil in the cooling water generally indicates the leakage of oil into the cooling system and leakage of water into the sump. The leakage may be slight. Slack cylinder head bolts may cause the trouble; it may also be due to a blown cylinder head gasket or to a distorted cylinder head.

3.4 The Radiator

The radiator filler cap contains a valve which seals the cooling system up to a pre-determined pressure (from 7 to 13 P.S.I., depending on the model). The effect of this is to raise the boiling point of the water and allow the engine to run at a higher temperature, which increases engine efficiency.

NEVER remove the radiator cap if the water boils. If it is necessary to remove the cap when the engine is hot, place a thick cloth over it and turn it very slowly anti-clockwise. This will reduce the pressure slowly. Unless these precautions are taken the cap will blow off immediately it becomes free and boiling water will be ejected from the radiator.

The cap is also fitted with a vacuum release valve to prevent the system being subjected to external pressure when the engine cools. A defective cap must be renewed.

Water Level: Check the water level daily and top up as required. The level is correct when the water is about 1 in. (2·5 cm) below the base of the filler neck.

Draining: Two draining points are provided—a tap on the base of the radiator and a plug on the right hand side of the cylinder block adjacent to the rear core plug. To drain the system first remove the radiator cap then turn on the tap at the base of the radiator ; next unscrew the plug at the cylinder block.

Make sure the plug is securely replaced and the tap turned off before re-filling the system. Remember anti-freeze if appropriate.

Flushing: Remove the filler cap and open both draining points. Ensure water is flowing freely and if not insert stiff wire to clear obstruction. Allow water to run through radiator until draining water is clear.

If the radiator is badly choked it may be reversed flushed by inserting the end of a water hose in the bottom radiator to cylinder block connecting hose, using a makeshift connection. Water will then overflow from the filler opening and the engine should be protected with plastic sheeting.

A radiator blocked with 'Fur', lime deposited from water, will cause over heating because of the reduced circulation. The only remedy is to use one of the 'Fur' removers sold by accessory stores. Unfortunately when used in a very old car they often uncover holes and a leaky radiator results.

3.5 The Fan Belt

To Adjust: Slacken off the two dynamo mounting bolts (one adjacent to the pulley and the other at the corresponding position at the rear of the dynamo). Slacken the adjustment retaining bolt in the slotted arm. The mounting bolts are best just slightly released, no more than enough to allow the dynamo to be moved and to remain in the position to which it is moved.

Pull the dynamo away from the engine. This will tighten the drive belt. Tension is correct when the up-and-down free movement in the belt at the mid-point of the length between

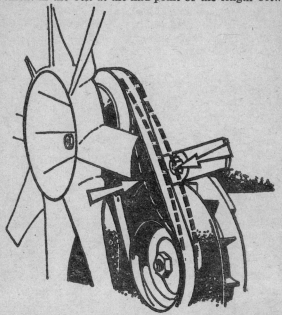

Fig. 9. Adjusting the fan/dynamo drive belt. The total movement of the belt between the arrows should be ½ in. The dynamo may be moved to adjust the belt if the bottom mounting bolts and the bolt in the slotted strap are slackened. The bolts are re-tightened after adjustment.

the dynamo and fan pulleys is ½ in. (1·3 cm). Check the adjustment after all the fixings have been re-tightened. See Fig. 9.

To Remove the Belt: Release the dynamo fixings as described above. Push the dynamo as far as possible towards the engine to obtain maximum slack in the belt. It will then be possible to press the belt sideways off the pulley. Turning the pulley will assist this action. Do not attempt to lever the belt off without slackening it. To do this will place excessive loads on the bearings.

On engines with plastic fans it is possible to damage the fan, if undue force is used but with the belt off the fan pulley it can be displaced from the other pulleys and *then* lifted clear of the fan.

A new belt is fitted by reversing the removal procedure, finally adjusting the belt correctly as described earlier.

3.6 The Thermostat

The thermostat is fitted below the water outlet on the top of the cylinder head.

The thermostat is closed when the engine is cold but is by-passed by a small bore pipe which allows limited circulation. As the engine warms up the thermostat opens progressively until at normal operating temperature the whole of the water flow is through the thermostat. In this way the engine is brought to operating temperature quickly.

The thermostat used is of the wax type and commences to open at 185°–192°F (85°–89°C). It is fully open at 210°–216°F (99°–102°C).

To Remove the Thermostat: First drain the system at least to below the top hose connection. Release the clip securing the hose to the outlet on top of the cylinder head. Take out the two bolts securing the outlet to the head and remove the outlet. The thermostat is located in the outlet by a circlip, which must be removed before the thermostat can be lifted out.

Testing the Thermostat: The thermostat may be tested by immersing it in water heated to the temperature range quoted above. Suspend the thermostat in the water so that it does not touch any part of the container. Heat the water from cold. Use a thermometer to ascertain the rise in temperature. The thermostat should open at the temperature quoted and close at the correct temperature as the water cools.

3.7 The Water Pump

The water pump or impellor requires no lubrication or other maintenance. After long service it should be inspected for water leakage. If leakage is present a replacement pump should be fitted. Special tools are required to dismantle and re-assemble the pump and therefore its repair is not normally feasible for the car owner.

4
The Electrical System

4.1 General
The 12 volt system has a negative earth connection. The generator is mounted on the engine and is belt driven from the crankshaft pulley. The battery is charged via a 3 bobbin regulator unit, which varies the charging rate according to the needs of the battery, the maximum current being restricted to a safe value to protect the generator from overload under certain conditions.

A conventional charge warning light is mounted on the instrument facia. This light illuminates immediately the ignition is switched on and indicates that the generator is charging by remaining out when the engine is running.

The ignition system comprises the usual distributor, coil and sparking plug arrangement. An oil filled ignition coil is used with current feed from the ignition switch through a resistor lead. This lead is shorted out by a connection between coil and starter solenoid when the starter control is operated, full battery voltage being applied to the coil while the starter is operating.

The starter motor may be of the pre-engaged type or inertia engaged type.

4.2 Dynamo
The dynamo fitted as standard is a Lucas C-40. The Lucas C-40L, which has a higher output is available at option.

4.3 Dynamo Fault Symptoms
  (1) The charge warning light does not go out as the engine speed rises.
  (2) The battery becomes discharged.

4.4 Causes and Cures

(1) The dynamo belt may be slack or broken (see 3.5, p. 50).
If the drive belt is in order there must be a fault in the
dynamo, control box or battery (see 4.5 below, 4.21, p. 67,
4.23, p. 70).
(2) This may be due to a fault in the battery, therefore see
4.21, p. 67, otherwise see (1) above.

4.5 To Check if the Dynamo is Charging

Disconnect the two leads on the dynamo. Note that these leads
must be re-connected in exactly the same positions from
which they were removed. Connect the two dynamo terminals
together with a piece of copper wire then connect this wire
to one test lamp lead (see 4.30, p. 73). Connect the other test
lamp lead to a good earth point. Start the engine and increase
the engine revs very slowly while watching the bulb. It
should be possible to light a high wattage bulb to full brilliance. If it is, it proves that the dynamo is charging but it
does not prove that it will deliver its full output, though it
probably will. Keep the revs down when you make the test
because the generator voltage is not controlled and will blow
the bulb if the r.p.m. are allowed to rise too high.

If the bulb fails to light during this test, the dynamo is
faulty and should be removed from the car for examination.
Do not use high r.p.m. to try and light the bulb. High revs
are likely to damage the dynamo windings, and these may be
sound even if the dynamo will not charge.

If you have a moving coil voltmeter with a full scale de-
flection of, say 10 to 30 volts, you can check the dynamo
with this meter. Connect the voltmeter between the bare copper wire as mentioned above and some earth point. Start the
engine and *carefully* increase engine r.p.m. to about 1000
r.p.m. (not higher). The voltmeter reading should rise
steadily with engine speed to about 25 volts. *Do not allow the
reading to exceed this figure* or the dynamo may be damaged.
Do not use high r.p.m. to try and obtain the reading.

If a correct reading is obtained the dynamo may be
assumed to be in order; if not the dynamo is faulty. If a correct reading is obtained, remove the bare copper wire and
refit the dynamo wires. Note that in connecting the voltmeter
correct polarity must be observed, negative meter lead to
earth.

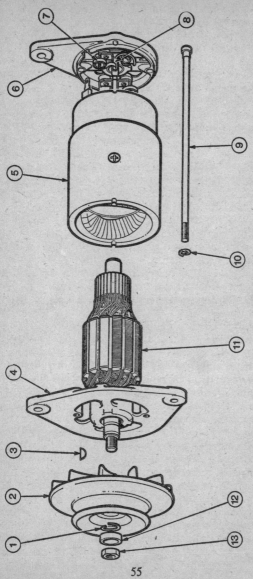

Fig. 10. The dynamo.

Key: 1. Spring washer; 2. Pulley; 3. Woodruff key; 4. Drive end bracket; 5. Yoke; 6. Commutator end bracket; 7. Brush spring; 8. Brush; 9. Long bolt; 10. Spring washer; 11. Armature; 12. Spacer; 13. Nut.

4.6 How to Remove the Dynamo from the Car
(1) Disconnect the battery earth terminal.
(2) Detach the dynamo leads.
(3) Release the three dynamo fixings. Push the dynamo to-
     wards the cylinder block so as to slacken the drive
     belt. Remove the drive belt from the dynamo pulley.
(4) Remove the three fixing bolts, supporting the dynamo
     while this is being done, then lift the dynamo away.

4.7 Notes on Re-fitting the Dynamo
The dynamo is re-fitted by reversing the removal procedure.
After the dynamo has been fitted the drive belt must be correctly adjusted (see 3.5, p. 50). The leads must be re-connected
in the correct order.

4.8 Dismantling the Dynamo
(1) Look at Fig. 10. Remove the drive pulley retaining nut.
     To do this it is necessary to hold the pulley. This can
     be done by placing the blade of a long screwdriver
     down the back of the pulley, between the vanes and
     holding the pulley stationary while the nut is unscrewed.
     Take care not to lose the Woodruff (curved base) key,
     since this must be refitted with the pulley (Fig. 10,
     item 3).
(2) Remove the two long bolts holding on the dynamo end
     plates. Take off the commutator end plate (Fig. 10, item
     6). It may be found necessary to free the plate by tap-
     ping the edge with a soft faced hammer. Detach the
     screws holding the brushes.
(3) Withdraw the remaining end plate, complete with the
     armature. No further dismantling is required for clean-
     ing and inspection.

4.9 Inspection and Repair
Repair is restricted to replacement of worn brushes and cleaning and under-cutting the commutator insulation. The commutator should be clean and bright. It may be cleaned by
gripping it in a piece of clean cloth moistened with petrol
and then turning it backwards and forwards. The cleaned
copper surface should be free from burning or pitting. If discoloured and/or pitted, the armature should be gripped lightly
in a vice and the commutator cleaned with fine glass paper.

This is best done by cutting a strip of the glass paper about the width of the commutator, looping it round the commutator with the rough side facing the copper segments and then pulling the ends of the strip backwards and forwards. The position of the armature in the vice should be changed frequently as the rubbing with the glass paper proceeds so that the cleaning is carried out evenly all round the commutator. *Do not use emery paper instead of glass paper.*

This treatment will remove slight pitting. If it is found that the surface of the commutator cannot be smoothed by this method, the only answer is to have the commutator skimmed in a lathe. In whatever way the commutator is smoothed it will be necessary to undercut the insulation between the com-

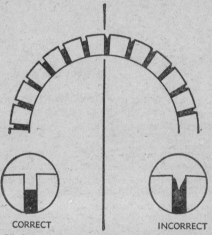

CORRECT   INCORRECT

Fig. 11. Under cutting the dynamo commutator insulation.

mutator segments. This is best done with a piece of old hacksaw blade. Break a blade in half and grind down the teeth on the broken end until they are just wide enough to cut down into the insulation as shown in Fig. 11. A width of 0·04 in. (1·02 mm) is suitable. Undercut the insulation to a depth of 0·020 to 0·035 in. (0·51 to 0·89 mm). It is important that the insulation is cut properly as shown in Fig. 11. When cutting is complete smooth the surface of the commutator with the glass paper to remove any burrs that the undercutting has produced, then blow away all dust.

Examine the armature for damage, such as signs of burning (which you may also smell) or signs of the armature rubbing on the pole pieces. The presence of any of these faults will mean that the dynamo requires a complete overhaul. Overheating may result in wires becoming detached from the commutator due to the solder melting. When this has occurred the dynamo may work again if the wires are soldered back into position.

There should be no slack in the armature shaft bearings. The shaft runs in a ball bearing at the drive end and a plain

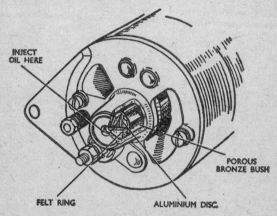

INJECT
OIL HERE

POROUS
BRONZE BUSH

FELT RING

ALUMINIUM DISC

Fig. 12. Dynamo lubrication.

bearing at the other end. Slack in any of these bearings means that an overhaul is required.

The brushes should be completely free in their holders. A tight brush or brushes will prevent the dynamo from charging. If there is any sign of tightness rub the sides of the brushes on a fine file or with a piece of the finest glass paper, finally checking that each brush is quite free to move in its holder. The minimum brush length is 0·25 in. (6·35 mm). Brushes worn down to near this length should be renewed. Make sure that the brush connections are clean and tight. If new brushes are fitted they will have to be bedded down to the surface of the commutator. This is explained below.

The method used in bedding down brushes is to cut a strip

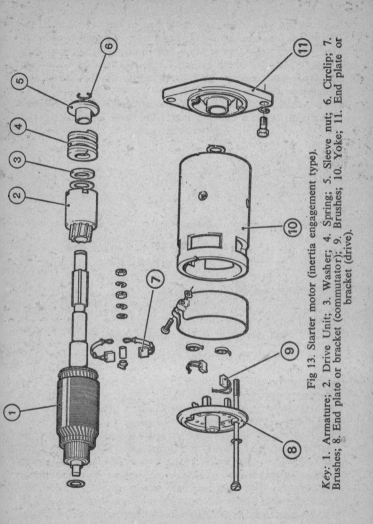

Fig 13. Starter motor (inertia engagement type).

Key: 1. Armature; 2. Drive Unit; 3. Washer; 4. Spring; 5. Sleeve nut; 6. Circlip; 7. Brushes; 8. End plate or bracket (commutator); 9. Brushes; 10. Yoke; 11. End plate or bracket (drive).

of fine glass paper about the same width as the commutator. The strip should be several inches long, so that it can be pulled backwards and forwards by pulling on its ends. The strip is placed on the commutator with the rough side up. Fit the end plate to the shaft and place the brushes in their holders with the brush springs. (Fig. 10, item 7) in position on top of the brushes. You may find it more convenient to do one brush at a time. Have someone hold the end plate or grip it lightly in the jaws of a vice. The end of the brush must press on to the glass paper, which is held tightly against the surface of the commutator. By alternately pulling on each end of the strip of glass paper the paper moves and seats the end of the brushes so that they conform to the curve of the commutator surface. When both brushes are properly bedded in, the commutator and other parts should be cleaned; then lightly oil the end of the armature shaft and re-assemble the dynamo.

Re-fit the dynamo to the car and properly tension the drive belt (see 3.5, p. 50).

Start the engine and observe if the ignition warning light goes out as the engine speed increases. If not, carry out the checks explained in 4.5, p. 54. If the result is negative there is a fault in the dynamo windings.

4.10 Dynamo Lubrication

The dynamo armature bearing requires occasional lubrication. Inject two drops of engine oil into the central hole, using an oil can. See Fig. 12.

4.11 The Starter

Inertia or pre-engaged starters are fitted. See Figs 13 and 14. In the inertia type starter engagement is effected by the acceleration of the starter shaft causing the pinion to move axially on a spiral and thus engage the starter ring teeth on the flywheel. The spiral also causes the starter pinion to 'wind in' and thus maintain the engagement so long as the starter is driving the engine. When the engine starts, however, its speed, through the gearing, is higher than that of the starter and the starter pinion is therefore rapidly wound in the opposite direction and moves back along the spiral and out of engagement.

The pre-engagement starters do not rotate until after the

pinion has engaged with the flywheel gear teeth. When the starter is operated a fork actuated by a solenoid moves the pinion towards the flywheel teeth. If tooth to tooth abutment occurs, preventing engagement, the pinion is arrested and is then caused to turn by the action of a spiralled sleeve, on which it is mounted, this turning enabling the pinion to engage. At the point when engagement is complete a pair of contacts close the starter circuit and the starter commences to drive the engine.

The starter pinion remains in engagement when the engine starts and is not withdrawn until the starter button is released. A roller clutch is incorporated in the starter drive which will transmit drive only from the starter to the engine and not from the engine to the starter so that the starter cannot be overspeeded when the engine starts. This system avoids the considerable shock that occurs when the inertia starter engages. It therefore reduces wear and noise.

The starters used are: Lucas M3.5G, Lucas pre-engaged M3.5G, Lucas pre-engaged M3.5J and Lucas pre-engaged M100.

4.12 Fault Symptoms

(1) Motor fails to operate—makes no sound.
(2) Motor makes a whirring noise but does not turn engine.
(3) Motor turns engine slowly and soon stops.
(4) Motor operates but is very noisy.
(5) Motor jams in engagement.
(6) Starter continues to turn engine when starter switch is released.

4.13 Causes and Cures

(1) Battery completely discharged. Switch on lights; if charged the battery should light the lights to full brilliance without fading. There may be a broken or disconnected wire. Check that the battery connections are sound; if in doubt remove, clean and replace the connections. The solenoid switch may be at fault. To check, disconnect the starter lead from the solenoid switch, leaving all other leads in place. With the ignition switched 'On' connect a test lamp (see 4.30, p. 73) between the starter lead terminal on this switch and any good earth point. When the starter switch on the dash is operated the test lamp should light, if it does not, there is a fault in

the solenoid switch, the key operated dash switch, or in the wiring. If the test lamp does light there is a fault in the starter or in the connection to it.

The starter motor brushes may be jammed in their holders so that they do not touch the commutator. The brushes may be excessively worn and need renewal. There may be a short circuit in the starter. These faults can only be determined and remedied by dismantling the starter. The starter may be jammed in engagement, see (5) overleaf.

(2) This may be due to a nearly discharged battery or, on an inertia engagement model, to the starter pinion sticking on the spiralled sleeve. Remove the starter from the car and clean the spiral by pouring a small quantity of petrol on the sleeve and operating the mechanism by turning the starter pinion, so causing it to move along the spiral. Any burrs due to wear should be filed away. Petrol is dangerous! Have less than a cupful exposed at any time and all containers securely sealed. There must be no flame nearer than 20 yards. The brushes may be worn or sticking.

(3) This is nearly always the sign of a discharged battery (see 4.21, p. 67). Check battery connections, remove, clean and replace. The cable connections may be loose or corroded, check all cable connections. The starter brushes may be excessively worn or sticking in their holders.

(4) Usually due to general wear. Noisy engagement may be caused by worn starter ring teeth.

(5) The inertia starter may jam in engagement and fail to operate. Usually a jammed starter may be freed by engaging 2nd or 3rd gear and rocking the car backwards and forwards (handbrake and ignition 'Off'). Failure of a pre-engaged starter to disengage is likely to be due to a faulty retraction spring. A bent starter shaft will cause the starter to jam in engagement, the only remedy in this case being a replacement starter.

(6) This would be due to a faulty starter switch or solenoid switch. If this occurs, to stop the starter, disconnect the battery.

4.14 Pre-engaged Starter: Pinion Adjustment
On some pre-engaged starters there is an adjustment for the pinion clearance. The adjustment is illustrated by Fig. 15. Adjust as follows:

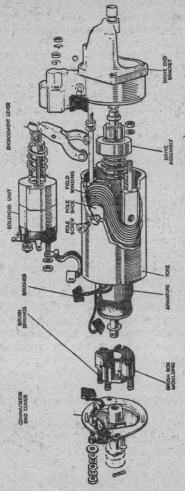

Fig. 14. Starter motor (pre-engagement type).

(1) Energize the shunt winding by connecting a 6 volt supply (12 battery in series with a 6 volt headlamp will do), between the starter body and the small terminal on the end of the solenoid.

(2) Take up any slack by pressing the pinion back towards the armature.

(3) Rotate the adjusting bolt as required to obtain the clearance shown between the pinion face and the thrust collar. Use a feeler gauge to measure the gap. Tighten the locknut while holding the adjuster stationary with a screwdriver. It should be noted that the adjustment arc is 180°. The arrow on the head of the adjuster must point towards the arrow on the drive end bracket.

4.15 Removing the Starter from the Engine

The starter may be removed by detaching the heavy cable from the connection on the starter (having first disconnected the battery earth lead) and removing the bolts holding the starter to the engine.

4.16 Inspecting the Starter

The starter will not work properly and may not work at all if the brushes are tight in their holders or if the commutator is dirty. Therefore when the starter has been taken off the car the inspection band should be removed (there is no inspection band on some pre-engaged starters). Removal of the band gives access to the brushes. Each brush should be removed from its holder after first lifting the spring with a piece of wire hooked at the end. Deal with only one brush at a time, replacing one before removing another. The brush should be quite free in its holder and not show signs of appreciable wear. A brush that is well down in its holder is excessively worn and should be replaced. When lifting the spring to release the brush note if the spring tension is weak (compare with another spring). Springs sometimes become annealed (soft) through overheating. Weak springs should be renewed.

Clean the commutator by pressing a small piece of clean, petrol damped cloth against it while the armature is turned. The inspection band may now be re-fitted and the starter replaced on the engine. If the starter still fails to work it should again be removed from the engine and dismantled for further inspection.

4.17 Dismantling the Starter Motor (Inertia Type)

(1) Refer to Fig. 13. Unscrew the bolt securing the inspection band and remove the band.

(2) Bend a piece of strong wire so that one end is hooked. Use the hooked end of the wire to lift the brush springs. While the springs are lifted in this way, pull the brushes (Fig. 13, item 9) out of their holders.

(3) Unscrew and remove the nuts and washers from the terminal to which the starter lead was attached. Unscrew and remove the two long bolts passing through the starter. Remove the drive end bracket, Fig. 13, item 11.

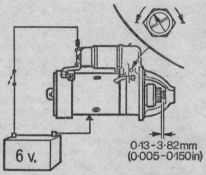

Fig. 15. Starter motor (pre-engagement type: pinion adjustment).

(4) The commutator end bracket may now be withdrawn, complete with the armature.

4.18 Repairing the Starter Motor (Inertia Type)

It has already been stated that worn brushes and/or weak brush springs should be replaced. Examine the armature for damage, a bent shaft or coils protruding from their slots. The former fault is caused by the engine 'kicking back' when the starter is engaged. The latter fault is due to overspeeding of the starter because of failure of the starter pinion to disengage when the engine starts. If the engagement mechanism on the drive shaft is damaged or worn it should be renewed. Check for play in the bearings. When the starter is assembled there should be no up-and-down play in the shaft. *Do not undercut the commutator segments.*

C

Brush Renewal: Unsolder the old brush tails from the earthed brush holders on the end plate or bracket and solder the tails of the replacement brushes in position. The other pair of brushes is soldered to the field winding.

The old brushes should be removed and the new ones soldered into position, but note that when the starter has an aluminium field winding it is impossible to solder the brush tails to the aluminium. Therefore the old tails must be cut to leave a short length in position to which the tail of the new brush may be soldered.

If, during inspection, it is found that the field coils, the armature or armature coils are damaged or the bearings worn a replacement starter should be fitted.

4.19 To Dismantle the Inertia Drive

Compress the spring and remove the circlip (or split pin and nut on the older models) see Fig. 13. Remove the large spring and barrel assembly from the motor shaft and screw the spiralled sleeve out of its nut. The other parts and return spring may then be removed. On re-assembly the drive may be tested by connecting the starter to a battery, the body of the starter being connected to the negative battery terminal (or positive battery terminal on positive earth pre-1966 cars). A heavy cable must be used to connect the starter terminal or it will not work. The starter body may be held against the battery terminal. This, of course, is also a test for the starter.

4.20 How to Test the Starter Solenoid Switch

With the ignition switched 'On' and the starter switch held in the 'Start' position the starter solenoid should be heard to operate if the ear is placed not far from it. It should also be possible to feel the solenoid operate if the hand is placed on it while the starter switch is operated. If the solenoid does not seem to operate and the fuse is sound check with the test lamp connected between the black/red wire connection on the solenoid and a good earth connection on the starter body. The bulb should light when the ignition/starter switch is 'On'. If it does not there is a fault in the ignition/starter switch or in the wire connecting the solenoid switch to it. Check that the white/black wire shows a good earth connection. The black/red feed wire should always be alive to earth. The heavy starter wire connected to the solenoid should become alive to earth when the starter/ignition switch is in the 'Start' position.

4.21 Battery: Fault Symptoms

(1) The battery is discharged—will not operate the starter. When the headlights are switched on they dim or will not light.

(2) Battery will charge, when placed on charger, but will not retain charge.

(3) The specific gravity (see (7) below) reading is low, even after the battery has been on charge for some time.

(4) The battery requires very frequent topping-up.

(5) Electrolyte discoloured.

(6) Battery polarity reversed.

(7) Battery charge remains low.

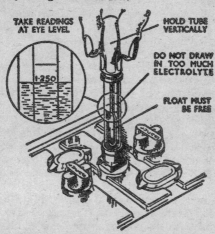

Fig. 16. Using a hydrometer to check the specific gravity of the battery acid. The acid level must be maintained $\frac{1}{4}$ in. above the tops of the separators.

4.22 Causes and Cures

(1) Lights, ignition, defroster left on all night. Dynamo not charging (see 4.5, p. 54). Battery stored for long period without being charged. Battery faulty (see (7) below).

(2) Check the acid level (see (7) below). The usual cause of this trouble is a faulty battery.

(3) Usually due to a faulty battery.

(4) When a lot of distilled water has to be added to a battery to maintain the correct level this is usually due to a faulty control box, which is causing the battery to receive too heavy a charge. This is bad and should be remedied as soon as possible. Look for a cracked battery case, especially if only one cell is affected.

(5) When the normally clear battery electrolyte becomes brown, this is a sign that the plates are disintegrating. The only remedy is a new battery.

(6) If a battery is connected up to a charger the 'wrong way round', that is with the positive terminal of the battery charger connected to the negative terminal of the battery, the battery polarity will be reversed. Such a battery will discharge very quickly and may cause itself damage. But it can usually be recharged later, correctly. A similar result will occur if a battery is connected to the car the wrong way round, the battery finally ending up with incorrect polarity.

If the polarity of a battery is reversed it should be first completely discharged by fitting it to the car, switching on the headlights and leaving them on until they are nearly out. The battery should then be fully charged by connecting it correctly to a battery charger.

Battery polarity may become reversed by a reversal of the dynamo polarity. If an ammeter is fitted it will show reversed polarity by indicating a charge reading when the lights are switched on and the engine stopped. If no ammeter is fitted one may be temporarily connected in the unearthed battery lead.

(7) This is usually due to a faulty battery. If continued charging will not bring the charge up, it may be due to a very low acid level which may, in turn be due either to a cracked battery case, or to neglect. In either case a new battery will be required.

It may be because of the way the car is used. If the car is parked for long periods with the parking lights on, the battery will run down. Low speed night driving will have a similar effect, as will frequent use of the starter either because the engine does not start properly or because a very large number of engine starts are required in the course of a day. Conditions of operation such as these prevent the battery charge rising properly and of course the trouble is greatly aggravated by cold weather. The remedy, if hard starting is the trouble, is to have the fault rectified. A home charger is a great help, particularly during the winter months, in ensuring that the battery is always in a fully charged condition.

If none of the above faults are present in rare instances there may be a leakage in the system that is causing the battery to run down. Such a leakage may be detected by means of an ammeter connected in series with the battery. To do this disconnect the unearthed battery lead from the battery. Hold the lead near the battery terminal from which it was removed and bridge the gap with the ammeter, that is place one ammeter lead on the battery terminal and the other on the battery cable connection. The meter must be connected the 'right way round', positive (+ or red) to the battery. *All switches must be off.* No reading should be obtained under these conditions. If a high reading is obtained a fault in the battery is indicated. Note that if an electric clock or alternator is fitted a very low discharge reading, of a few milliamps, is always present, but is in fact less than the normal internal discharge rate of the wiring. You are looking for something rather greater than this, say in excess of 50 milliamps.

Check the acid level (see Fig. 16 and further below) and if this is right switch on the headlights and operate the starter. If the battery is sound it will 'spin' the engine energetically and while the lights will dim slightly when the starter is operated they will not dim right down if the battery is in good condition. When the battery begins to go the starter usually gives warning, the symptom being most evident after an overnight rest. Once the starter turns the engine sluggishly and the lights dim right down when it is being used, the battery is either faulty or is in a low state of charge.

A battery may become faulty by being stored for a few months without receiving freshening-up charging. If stored for long periods without charging the battery will slowly lose its charge and the plates become sulphated. Any sulphation will greatly reduce the battery capacity and much of it will render the battery unsuitable for further use.

Check the gravity of the acid with a hydrometer (see Fig. 16). The specific gravity indicates the state of charge of the battery, as shown below:

Take a reading from each cell in turn, returning the acid to the cell after the specific gravity reading has been obtained. Do not transfer acid from one cell to another.

A fully charged battery should give a reading of between 1·240 and 1·260. A reading of 1·200 indicates that the battery is discharged.

The acid level should be $\frac{1}{4}$ in. (6·2 mm) above the top of the plates. If it is low add distilled water to correct it, then charge the battery for not less than one hour before taking the readings. If the reading of one or two cells is slightly less than the others a prolonged charge should correct this ; if it does not the cells are faulty. If when the battery should be fully charged individual cells differ by more than 0·050 the battery is faulty and should be renewed.

If a low reading is obtained the battery should be placed on charge. Allowing a battery to stand in a discharged or partially discharged condition will encourage sulphation.

Do not under any circumstances add pure sulphuric acid to a cell in an attempt to increase the gravity reading.

4.23 The Control Box

The control box is a Lucas unit with three bobbins to give both voltage and current regulation. This combination allows the unit to give a high charge rate to a very low battery, so as to bring it up to a fully charged condition quickly, but without risk of overloading the dynamo. As the battery becomes charged the charging current is tapered off to a constant low value when the battery becomes fully charged.

The control box also contains the cut-out, which automatically switches the battery out of circuit when the dynamo is running at too low a speed to charge it, and thus prevents the battery discharging through the dynamo under these conditions. As soon as the dynamo speed is high enough to provide a sufficient voltage to charge the battery, the cut-out switches the battery into circuit.

In general, the private owner should replace a control box that proves to be faulty or incorrectly adjusted, or trust readjustment to an auto-electrician.

4.24 Fault Symptoms
(1) **Ignition warning light remains on when the engine speed rises.**

(2) The ignition warning light goes out as the engine speed rises, then goes on again and as the engine speed rises further, goes out again.

(3) The ignition warning lamp lights very brilliantly as the engine speed rises

(4) Battery requires frequent topping-up.

(5) Battery becomes discharged.

(6) Ignition light remains 'ON' when engine is stopped and ignition has been switched 'OFF'.

4.25 Causes

(1) This indicates that the cut-out points are not closing, either due to a fault in the cut-out or in the generator.

(2) The cut-out is cutting in too late and requires adjustment.

(3) this suggests that there is a high resistance at the cut-out points or a fault in the cut-out coils.

(4) The voltage/current regulators are incorrectly adjusted resulting in the battery being over charged.

(5) This may be due to a faulty battery (see 4.21, p. 67) or to a faulty generator (see 4.5, p. 54). There may be a wiring fault (see 4.20, p. 66). The cut-out points may not be closing.

(6) Cut-out points are not opening. *Disconnect the battery immediately.* If there are signs of burning, start the engine and run at fast tick-over while the battery is being disconnected.

No cures are given for the above faults because, in general, when a control box becomes faulty it is better to have it renewed.

4.26 Flashing Indicators: Fault Symptoms

(1) None of the indicators light when the indicator switch is operated.

(2) Only some of the indicator lights flash when the indicator switch is operated.

(3) The flashing rate is too high.

(4) The flashing rate is too low.

(5) All the indicator lights illuminate continuously without flashing.

4.27 Causes and Cures

(1) May be caused by a blown fuse or faulty flasher unit. The indicator switch may be faulty. Check if the other auxiliaries

work. If they do the fuse must be sound. If the auxiliaries do not work, the fuse is blown and should be renewed, see below. It is assumed that the battery is properly connected up and is charged. If the fuses are in order either the wiring is faulty (see 4.29 below) or the flasher unit is on open circuit.

If the fuse is found to have blown, fit a new fuse with the indicators and all auxiliaries switched off. Switch indicators on one side on. If the fuse blows there is a fault in the wiring to this side or in the flasher. If the fuse does not *blow*, move the indicator switch to operate the other side. If the fuse now blows this indicates that there is a fault in this part of the flasher wiring. If the flashers are working normally, it may be that the fuse was blown by a fault in one of the other auixiliary circuits so switch them on one by one and note the one that blows the fuse. This will localize the fault. A fuse box is mounted on the engine rear bulkhead and it contains six (or on some models 7) fuses—a diagram on the box cover identifying the position of each fuse. See also 4.52, p. 94.

(2) If the faulty indicator lamps are both on the same side, this is probably a wiring fault, so check the wires and their connectors. It is just possible that both bulbs are blown therefore each bulb should be checked (see 4.34, p. 77). If only one of the lights fails this will normally be a blown bulb, but if the bulb proves to be sound there is a fault in the wiring.

(3) This may be a fault in the flasher unit, but it may also be due to the fitting of incorrect bulbs, so check that the correct wattage bulb is fitted.

(4) This may be due to a fault in the flasher unit or to the bulbs fitted having too low a wattage.

(5) This is normally a fault in the flasher unit. Test the unit as explained below.

4.28 How to Test the Flasher Unit

A quick way to test the flasher unit is to connect the two posts on the flasher together with a piece of bare copper wire without removing the push-on connectors, though they may be pulled up a little to fit the wire. With the wire in position, and the ignition switched on the direction indicator lights should illuminate continuously on one side or the other, depending on which way the indicator switch is moved. If this occurs the flasher is faulty. If the lights do not do this use the test lamp to check if the push-on connector on the white wire is alive to earth when the ignition switch is on. If it is there is a fault in the wiring to the direction indicator switch or in the switch itself. If the connector is not alive to earth there is a fault in the wiring to the ignition switch or in the switch itself.

If a blown switch was associated with the failure of the unit, this would indicate a possible short circuit in the wiring and if this is so a new flasher unit must not be fitted until the

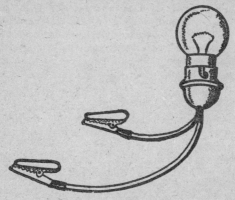

Fig. 17. The test lamp.

short circuit is cleared otherwise it will be destroyed. Remember to remove the wire connected across the flasher posts.

4.29 How to Trace Wiring Faults

Wiring faults can be broadly divided into three kinds: short circuits, in which fuses blow and there may be burning; broken wires or detached connections, and bad contacts in cable connectors or elsewhere. Poor contacts may prevent components working properly without preventing them working altogether.

4.30 Test Lamp.

A very simple way of testing electrical circuits is to use a test lamp. This can be made very easily (see Fig. 17). Wire up a suitable bulb holder with two flying leads, two strands of plastic covered flex will do very well. The bulbs used must of course be 12 volt bulbs, to suit the car battery voltage. It is convenient to fit a crocodile clip to the end of each of the wires. A clip may also be placed on a pocket screwdriver, close to the handle, the screwdriver then being used as a probe to check various points by touching them.

It is an advantage to have two such test bulbs, one fitted with a headlamp bulb and one fitted with a tail type bulb. This is because for some jobs it is necessary to draw a heavy current, e.g. when testing the dynamo, while in others a small current is best.

Because it is easier to find a holder for it the old type bayonet fitting headlamp bulb is best. If a modern type bulb is used it will probably be necessary to solder the wires on to the bulb, one to the metal flange and one to one of the bottom contacts.

4.31 How to Trace Short Circuits

The position of a short circuit is localized by the fuse which blows. If a fuse blows, is replaced and blows again the fault must be found and remedied. The test bulb should be clipped across the fuse holder clips. A voltmeter may be used instead of the test bulb. With the bulb or voltmeter connected, refer to the wiring diagram at the end of the book, and wires can be disconnected one by one in the circuit or circuits involved. The disconnections should be made only momentarily starting at the furthest point from the battery until one is found that puts the test bulb out or causes the meter to give a zero reading. If more than one wire is disconnected at the same time there may be difficulty in making sure that the wires can be replaced in their right positions.

The lighting circuits and ignition circuits are not fused. If a short circuit takes place that causes burning, it is possible that so much damage has been done to other wires that a whole loom needs replacement. However, if this has not happened and only one wire proves to be defective, the ends of the wire should be cut off and taped with insulating tape. A new wire, external to the wiring loom is then connected between the points which the faulty wire connected. The circuit should then work normally. It is necessary to make sure the new wire is held securely in position along the whole of its length, otherwise sooner or later it will give trouble.

4.32 How to Trace Open Circuits

These are caused by the ends of wires being pulled from their connections, or by terminal screws becoming loose. Corrosion sometimes causes an open circuit and this is one of the things to look for, especially in an old model. The trouble may occur at switches, in wire connectors, in fact, at any point where connections are made. It is usually only a matter of cleaning the parts and then connecting them up again. In

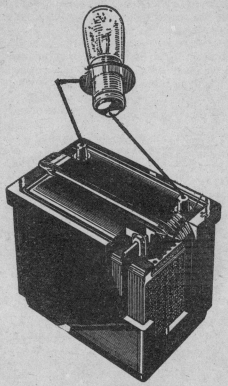

Fig. 18. Testing bulbs.

rare cases a wire may break and since this is a very well concealed fault only a continuity test of the wire involved will reveal it.

It is possible to check for continuity by looking for live points with the test lamp or voltmeter. The voltmeter or test lamp has one lead connected to the unearthed battery terminal while the other end of the lead is touched on the connecting point. The component may be a windscreen wiper motor, ignition coil, lamp or switch and so on. If current is present the lamp will light or the voltmeter will show a reading. When testing in this way the faulty circuit can be checked from point to point by reference to the wiring diagram at the end of the book, until the break in continuity is discovered. It is assumed the fuse has not blown.

Another method for tracing circuit faults is to use a loop wire to connect the two points and this is the best method to use when the faulty wire is not in the battery circuit. For example, if it is thought that there is a break in one of the wires connecting the dynamo to the control box these wires can be easily checked. The wire from the connection marked D on the control box goes to the D dynamo terminal, therefore both these points can be connected by a loop wire. The loop wire need only be a piece of single plastic covered lighting flex. The same can be done with the other dynamo wire, the one connecting the F terminal on the control box to the F terminal on the dynamo. A temporary connection is all that is necessary at first. Obviously if connecting any of these points with a loop wire makes the dynamo charge, then there must be a fault in the wire replaced by the loop. Other points may be dealt with in the same way, but be sure what points you are connecting and do not work haphazardly. Connecting an earth point to a live point by a loop wire will cause the loop wire to become red hot.

4.33 High Resistance (bad contacts) and Faulty Earth Connections

High resistance connections may occur at any point where wires are connected to switches or other components and in wire connectors. The trouble is most likely to occur in old cars. Wires held by screwed terminals or push-on connectors may become faulty. Any connections suspected should be parted, cleaned and re-connected. Simply parting and re-fitting a push-on connector several times will sometimes cure the fault, temporarily.

A common source of trouble with poor connections is the battery terminals. Occasionally it will be found that when all the electrical circuits are working normally an attempt to operate the starter puts them all off. This indicates that the battery connections need to be removed, cleaned and properly re-made. It is always worth while completely covering the battery connections with petroleum jelly, to protect them from corrosion.

Another kind of high resistance connection is the faulty earth. Where earthing connections are direct to the body a high resistance may build up leading to a disconnection. A good way to check a faulty earth connection is to take a pocket screwdriver and connect the blade to the end of a length of plastic flex. The insulation near the end of the flex must be removed so that the bared wire may be tightly wound round the screwdriver and then twisted to make a good connection. Connect the other end of the flex to the earthed battery terminal (but any good earth connection will do, if the battery itself is properly earthed) and touch the earth connection point on the component with the screwdriver. Pressure may be needed on a sharp corner of the blade to penetrate any paint or surface corrosion. If the original earth connection was at fault this will bring the circuit back to life. The controlling switch must be 'On' when the test is made. If a faulty earth is proved the connection should be removed, cleaned and re-made. An alternative remedy is to connect a new earth, a wire between the point that requires to be earthed and some good earth point.

4.34 Testing Bulbs

If you suspect that a bulb is faulty but are not sure it may be tested on a battery (see Fig. 18). Connect a short length of single plastic covered flex to one of the battery terminals. To test a bulb that has only one contact on its base, hold the bulb with the free end of the wire in contact with the metal side of the bulb while the contact on the bottom of the bulb is pressed on to the other battery terminal. The bulb will light if it is sound.

If the bulb has two contacts on the base, as headlamp and stop and tail bulbs do, hold the wire in contact with the metal side of the bulb as before, but allow only one of the base contacts to touch the battery terminal. This should light one of the bulb filaments. Now touch the other contact on the battery terminal, this should cause the other filament to light. If both filaments light the bulb is sound, if only one lights the bulb is faulty. Quite often a faulty filament can be seen to be broken on careful inspection, but this is not always possible.

If the test is made when the battery is connected in the car, the wire can be connected to any good earth point and the bulb contacts touched on the unearthed battery terminal, but the end of the wire must *not* be allowed to come into contact *directly* with the battery terminal. Connecting the two terminals of a battery together with a piece of wire constitutes a short circuit; the wire will become red hot and the hands may be burned.

4.35 Bulb Renewal

Headlamps. In some cars the lamps are fitted with sealed beam light units while in other cases bulb units are fitted. The removal instructions for each type are similar.

First remove the grille by taking out the 9 attachment screws and pulling the grille clear of the body. Disconnect the battery to obviate possible damage by an inadvertent short circuit.

If rectangular lamps are fitted to your Escort remove the 3 attachment screws holding the lamp unit in position and lift the unit clear. The connecting socket can now be pulled off to free the unit completely. This also gives access to the parking bulb, which may be depressed in its holder and then twisted free. When a headlamp bulb is fitted, this may be pulled from the reflector/lens unit.

If circular lamps are fitted to your Escort, after removing the grille as described earlier, take out the 3 screws holding the headlamp bezel (rim) and detach the bezel. The lamp unit may then be completely detached or the parking bulb removed, as previously described. When a headlamp bulb is fitted this may be pulled from the reflector/lens unit.

Replacing the units and bulbs is a reversal of the removal procedure.

Rear Lamps. To renew the stop and tail and direction indicator bulbs, first disconnect the battery to avoid risk of short circuit. Access to the rear of the lamp is required and this is obtained via the luggage compartment. Remove the lamp assembly cover panel by unscrewing the knurled retaining nut. The bulb holders may now be pulled out and the bayonet fitting bulbs removed.

Front Direction Indicator Lamps. Remove the two screws re-

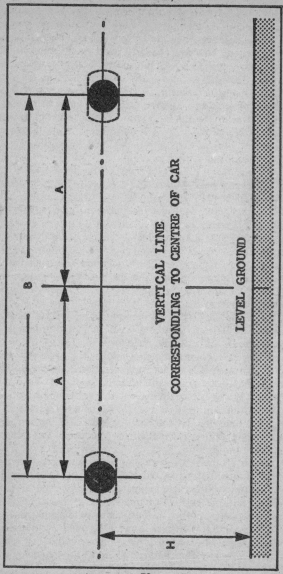

VERTICAL LINE
CORRESPONDING TO CENTRE OF CAR

LEVEL GROUND

Fig. 19. How to adjust the headlamp beams correctly.

taining the lamp rim in position and remove the rim and plastic lens. The bayonet fitting bulb may then be removed from its holder. When re-fitting the rim ensure the sealing gasket and lamp lens are properly located.

Rear Licence Plate Lamp. Disconnect the battery to prevent an inadvertent short circuit occurring. Take out the two screws attaching the lamp to the body. Remove the two lens attachment screws and remove the lens. The bulb may now be withdrawn.

Interior Light. Disconnect a battery lead to isolate battery. Very carefully prise the lamp cover out of the windscreen panel. The bulb may then be removed from its retainer.

4.36 Headlamp Beam Adjustment

In order to pass the MOT test, the headlamps must be correctly adjusted to avoid dazzle. Adjustment consists of moving the lamps vertically and horizontally by means of slotted adjusting screws until the correct beam angles are obtained. The screw for vertical adjustment is accessible through a hole on the top of the grille. The horizontal adjustment screw is accessible through a hole in the grille adjacent to the lamp rim. The lights are best adjusted at night or near dark. (See Fig. 19).

(1) Place the car facing a smooth wall and 10 ft. away from it. The car must be level, unloaded and at right angles to the wall. Bounce the car slightly to ensure it is settled on the suspension.

(2) Refer to Fig. 19. Measure the height H from the ground to the centre of the headlamps.

(3) Mark a vertical centreline on the wall so that it is in line with the vertical centreline of the car. Mark a horizontal line on the wall parallel with the ground. Distance H is the height of the centre of the headlamp above the ground.

(4) Switch on the headlamps and by means of the vertical and horizontal screws already mentioned, adjust each headlamp so that the centres of the brightest areas of the beams lie on the horizontal line 42·2 in. (107·2 cms) apart (distance B) and both equally distant from the vertical line (distance B is twice A).

NOTE: On early cars access to the headlamp adjusting screws is obtained by removing the grille.

4.37 The Ignition System

The ignition system is mainly conventional in that the interruption of the 12 volt primary coil circuit by the opening of the contact breaker points causes a high voltage pulse (in the region of 30,000 volts) to appear in the coil secondary circuit. This high voltage causes the current to jump across the gap between the spark plug points as a spark.

An oil filled coil is used. The high tension leads are special, a carbon impregnated rayon strand passing through the insulating covering instead of the usual core of fine wires. These special leads serve as ignition suppressors, therefore if renewal becomes necessary a set of leads should be obtained from a Ford agent.

It is a low voltage ignition coil. The feed to this coil is taken through a resistor lead, connected between the SW terminal on the coil and the ignition switch. When the starter switch is operated the resistor lead is shorted out, so that for the short period the starter is operating the full battery voltage appears across the coil which in consequence gives a very intense spark and thus counters the effect of the drop in battery voltage that takes place when the starter is operated. It is therefore essential that if a new coil-to-ignition switch wire is fitted, it must be the correct wire, obtained from a Ford agent. To fit an ordinary wire will cause the coil to burn out. However to meet an emergency it would be in order to fit a 12 volt coil and use a length of ordinary wire to connect the ignition switch to the coil.

4.38 Fault Symptoms

  (1) **Engine will not start.**
  (2) **Engine runs but is difficult to start.**
  (3) **Engine misfires.**
  (4) **Engine overheats.**
  (5) **Engine lacks power.**
  (6) **Engine knocks.**
  (7) **Engine kicks back when being started.**

4.39 Causes and Cures

(1) This may be an ignition fault. It may also be a fuel fault (see 2.2, p. 34). It may be a mechanical fault (see 1.2, p. 9). Make sure the ignition is switched 'On'. Check that the battery is in good condition (will give headlights normal brilliance). Inspect the coil and distributor connections for faults; move the wires with the hand to ensure that they are firmly attached.

High Tension Circuit Tests. Remove the distributor cap. It is held in position by two clips. Observe if the contact breaker points are closed. This is not always easy to tell. If in doubt move the points part (ignition 'On') and observe if there is a spark. If there is no spark the points are *not* closed; closed points will always give a small spark when they are opened. If the points are not closed close them by operating the starter with the ignition 'Off'. Alternatively the car can be pushed in top gear to turn the engine until the points are closed, but the ignition *must* be 'Off'.

Disconnect the lead from the coil to the distributor at the distributor end. Switch 'On' the ignition. Hold the end of the detached lead about a quarter of an inch (six millimetres) away from any conveniently situated metallic part. While holding the lead in this way, open the contact breaker points with a small screwdriver, a pocket knife or directly with the fingers. Alternatively have someone switch the ignition 'Off' and 'On' several times; the result will be the same as if the points were opened (provided they were closed in the first place). At the moment the points open or the circuit is 'opened' by the ignition switch a spark should jump from the end of the high tension lead to the metallic part near to it. Try once or twice. If there is no spark there is almost certainly a fault in the low tension circuit (see low tension circuit faults below). If there *is* a spark, hold the end of the lead about an eighth of an inch (three millimetres) away from the brass strip on the top of the rotor arm (ignition switched 'On'). *There should be no spark.* If there is a spark, the rotor arm is cracked and a new one must be fitted.

If the test is satisfactory (there is no spark), examine the distributor cap for cracks or 'tracking'. Tracking produces leakage lines over the interior surface of the distributor cap, due to dirt or moisture lowering the electrical resistance to the point where sparks can travel over it. Once made these marks will leak however well the surface is cleaned. In an emergency you can try rubbing out the leakage tracks with fine glass paper, or better, drilling a small hole (or holes) to interrupt the tracks. The ultimate only remedy is to fit a new distributor cap. Examine the carbon brush in the centre of the distributor cap, it may be broken or stuck up in the cap. Instead of the brush there may be a spring strip on top of the rotor which may be broken. The remedy for both these faults is obvious.

The only other HT fault likely to cause absence of a spark would be failure of the coil. Unfortunately a coil may fail in several ways; it may work normally until it heats up and then fail to produce a spark or spark erratically. When this happens the coil is often not suspected. If it goes completely dead this is easily discovered. If in any doubt about the coil the best thing to do is to temporarily fit a good one, possibly one borrowed from a friend, then if the new coil results in no improvement the old coil is good and can be used again. On the other hand if the new coil clears the trouble the old coil is faulty. Remember that if the ignition leads and/or distributor are moist this will prevent the plugs sparking. If a low tension fault is indicated proceed as explained below.

Low Tension Circuit Tests. We mentioned earlier how, if the contact breaker points are closed and are opened after the ignition is switched on a small spark should be seen. The presence of this spark indicates that current is flowing in the low tension circuit. Another way to make a test is to connect the test lamp (see 4.30, p. 73) across the coil terminals. With the lamp connected and the ignition switched 'On' turn the engine. If the circuit is in order the test lamp will light when the contact breaker points close and go out when the points *open*. If the lamp remains on all the time when the engine is turned, the contact breaker points are short circuited, probably due to incorrect assembly (see Fig. 22, p. 87). If the lamp fails to light at all and the ignition is switched 'On' with the battery connected and charged (good battery connections) there is a fault in the low tension wiring, in the ignition switch or in the coil. The fault is most likely in the wiring and least likely in the coil.

The fault could be caused by the contact breaker points not opening due to incorrect adjustment or to breakage of part of the moving arm so that it was no longer actuated by the cam. In odd cases the moving arm will stick on its pivot so that when opened by the cam it remains open. Dirt on the contact breaker points or something placed between the points will cause the fault. In this case the points should be removed and rubbed down on one of the carborundum slips sold for this purpose. Only a little light rubbing is necessary. The points are covered with a relatively thin coating of rare metal and if this is rubbed through the points are no longer serviceable. Faults in the wiring or the components associated with it may be traced as explained in 4.29 earlier in this chapter.

(2) This may be a carburettor fault (see 2.2, p. 34). Possible causes are dirty plugs and/or incorrect gap settings. The contact breaker points may be dirty or incorrectly set (see 4.45, p. 89).

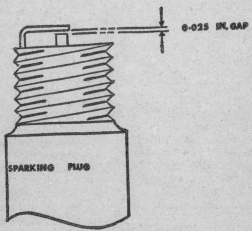

Fig. 20. How to measure sparking plug gaps.

Check the high tension leads to the plugs and coil. After some years the leads may become perished and leaky. If there is any doubt about the leads renew them all. Do not use ordinary HT wire as normally supplied by accessory stores or garages. The leads are special, with a carbon impregnated rayon core so to avoid trouble obtain the correct set of leads from a Ford Agent. *NOTE.* Because a coil of lower voltage than the battery is fitted, a resistor lead is used to connect the ignition switch to the coil. Damage would occur if this lead was replaced by a normal wire LT lead.

(3) Check for dirty or otherwise faulty plugs, possibly incorrectly set gaps. Check that the contact breaker points gap is correctly set (see 4.45, p. 89), and that the points are clean. The spring on the contact breaker moving arm may be broken, or the arm may be tight on its pivot. The ignition capacitor may be faulty. The contact breaker points gap will be found in 10.3, p. 144. Check all wire connections for tightness. Make sure that the leads from the distributor are connected to the correct plugs (see Fig. 21).

Tracking inside the distributor cap will cause trouble. Mis-

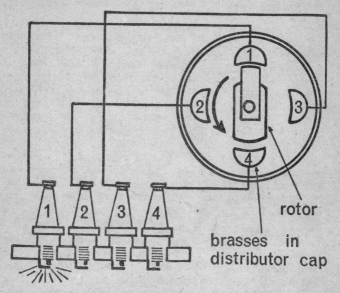

rotor

brasses in distributor cap

no. 1 plug sparking

Fig. 21. The correct order to connect the sparking plug leads.

firing may be caused by a mechanical fault (see 1.2, p. 9). The plug type may be incorrect, see 4.42 below.

(4) When due to the ignition this is usually caused by a retarded spark. Check the ignition timing as explained in 4.49, p. 90. The cause may be a fuel fault (see 2.2, p. 34). The engine may need to be decarbonised (see 1.4, p. 14).

(5) If an ignition fault this may be incorrect ignition timing.

Check the timing as explained in 4.49, p. 90. The cause may be binding brakes (see 7.4, p. 116). The fuel system may be at fault (see 2.2, p. 34). The engine may need to be decarbonised (see 1.4, p. 14).

(6) This may be due to excessive ignition advance. Check the timing as explained in 4.49, p. 90. The engine may need to be decarbonized (see 1.4, p. 14). The fault may be mechanical (see 1.2, p. 9).

(7) The ignition is too far advanced, correct as explained in 4.49, p. 90.

4.40 Sparking Plugs: Cleaning and Gap Setting

Cleaning: After long service the plugs become fouled up with carbon and must be cleaned. The only really satisfactory way of doing this is to use a plug cleaning machine. Carbon may be cleaned from the end of the plug with a wire brush but this is not sufficient, the interior of the plug must be cleaned. *Gap Setting:* See Fig. 20. After the plug has been cleaned, re-set the gap between the centre electrode and the electrode attached to the plug body to the correct gap given in 10.1, p. 144. Do this by bending the *outer electrode, not the centre electrode.* The blade of the feeler gauge should just push into the gap with slight drag, no force being needed but there being no play between the blade and the plug electrodes. Do not use the feeler gauge blade to bend the plug electrode.

4.41 To Test A Sparking Plug

Unscrew the plug from the engine. Place the plug, with its lead still attached so that the body is in contact with some convenient metallic part of the car or engine. It is assumed that the HT lead is connected to the plug by means of a plastic cap, otherwise the plug terminal must not touch anything. Start the engine. Keep the hands and elbows clear of the fan. If the engine will not start it will be sufficient to turn it with the starter (ignition switched 'on'). A bright blue spark should occur at regular intervals. It is not easy to see the spark in bright daylight or sunlight and it may be necessary to shade the points. If there is no spark, or the spark is weak and reddish, or if there is sparking within the body of the plug it needs to be cleaned or possibly renewed.

4.42 Sparking Plugs: General

Do not overtighten plugs. Do not use old plug washers, they

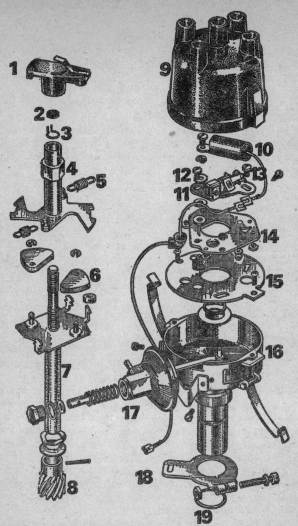

Fig. 22. The distributor. *KEY*: 1. Rotor. 2. Pad. 3. Clip. 4. Cam and shaft. 5. Spring. 6. Centrifugal weights. 7. Drive shaft. 8. Drive pinion. 9. Cap. 10. Capacitor. 11. Contact assembly. 12. Retaining screw. 13. Adjusting screw. 14. Upper plate. 15. Lower plate. 16. Body. 17. Suction advance/retard mechanism. 18. Clamp plate. 19. Oil seal.

do not make a gas-tight seal. Screw in the plug until it is finger tight on its seat, then tighten one half turn with a plug spanner.

Use only the recommended plugs (see 10.1, p. 144) or plugs of a similar heat range to those recommended. Remember plugs may *look* the same and yet be quite different. The use of incorrect plugs often gives rise to what seem to be mysterious misfiring troubles. Plugs of too low a heat range will misfire at wide throttle openings. Plugs of too high a heat range will misfire at low throttle openings.

4.43 Ignition Coil

A 'Ballast' ignition coil is used. This operates off a lower voltage than the battery voltage, the excess voltage being dropped by a 1·4–1·6 ohm resistor lead between the ignition switch and the coil. The reason for this is explained in 4.37, p. 81.

The ignition coil requires no maintenance, but the connections on the coil should be checked occasionally for tightness and should be maintained in a clean condition.

4.44 To Test the Ignition Coil

Coil failure is not common. When a fault in the coil does occur, it may be an open circuit in which case the coil goes completely dead and simple tests will soon locate the trouble as being in the coil. Sometimes the fault is intermittent. The coil may work properly for a time and then stop working and, after a while, it will work again. Sometimes the coil will work when it is cold and then fail completely when it is hot; the car starts and runs normally but after an interval the engine stops. Probably the quickest way to attack this problem is to fit a coil known to be good. If this clears the trouble the old coil is faulty and should be thrown away but if the trouble persists the old coil may be re-fitted, and the search for the fault continued. Otherwise effective checks can only be made on the coil immediately after the trouble has occurred, as explained below.

Turn the engine until the contact breaker points are open. Alternatively open the points by pressing on the moving arm and then pushing a thin piece of card between the points before releasing the arm. This effectively insulates the two points from each other and so breaks the low tension circuit.

Connect the test lamp (see 4.30, p. 73), or a voltmeter be-

88

tween the terminal on the coil marked SW and a good earth point. With the ignition switch 'On' the lamp should light normally. If a voltmeter is used it should register about 12 volts. If the lamp fails to light (or the voltmeter to give a reading) this means there is a fault in the wiring from the ignition switch to the coil, in the feed to the switch or in the ignition switch itself. If the test is satisfactory, remove the test lamp lead from the SW terminal on the coil and place it on the CB terminal. Now the current has to pass through the coil to light the lamp or operate the meter. The meter will give approximately the same reading, but the test bulb will burn noticeably less brightly if the low tension circuit within the coil is continuous. Failure of the lamp to light or meter to register would indicate a break in the low tension circuit within the coil. The only remedy is a replacement coil.

If both the above tests are satisfactory additional High Tension and Low Tension circuit tests described in 4.39, p. 81, should be made. Any fault should thus come to light.

4.45 Adjusting the Contact Breaker Points
(1) Slacken the retaining screw (12) Fig. 22, and the adjusting screw (13).
(2) The points must be fully open (moving arm heel on highest point on cam).
(3) Move the fixed contact as required to give the correct clearance between the points 0·025 in. (0·64 mm). This is the No. 25 blade on a feeler gauge set. When the clearance is correct the feeler gauge will move between the points with slight drag.
(4) When the gap is correct tighten screws (12) and (13). Re-check the clearance after the screws have been tightened.
(5) After adjustment apply a smear of grease to the cam face, and place two drops of light oil on the pad under the rotor.

4.46 To Remove the Contact Breaker Assembly
(1) Remove the distributor cap and rotor.
(2) Slack off the retaining screw ((12), Fig. 22) and pull out the two spade terminals below the screw to which the wires are attached.
(3) Completely remove both the retaining screw (12) and

adjusting screw (13). The contact assembly is now free and can be removed.

To replace the contact assembly reverse the above procedure.

4.47 Cleaning the Contact Breaker Points

The contact breaker points may be cleaned by separating them when closed and pushing a piece of thin clean card between them, moving this backwards and forwards once or twice and then withdrawing it. The card may be moistened with petrol. Do not use card made of soft material, since the surface of this may tear, leaving pieces between the points.

If thorough cleaning is required, the contact breaker assembly should be removed, see 4.46, and the surface of each point lightly rubbed with a contact file or abrasive slip. Very little rubbing is required. Excessive rubbing will remove the coating of rare metal on the points and they will then be useless. Sometimes the surfaces of the points become oxidised and then cause misfiring or even stoppage of the engine. This invariably happens if an excessive quantity of oil is used when lubricating the contact breaker. The remedy is to remove and clean the points as already explained. If the points re-oxidise soon after cleaning, this would indicate that there is a fault in the ignition capacitor, assuming that excessive oil is not still present.

4.48 Distributor

The distributor type fitted varies between the 1100 c.c., 1300 c.c. and GT models depending on whether the engine is high or low compression. The direction of rotation is anti-clockwise looking down on the rotor.

Centrifugal weights spring location and identification: The primary spring has the largest diameter across the coils, the secondary spring has the smallest diameter. Two advance slots are provided, one of which is marked 15L and one 10L. The secondary spring should be adjacent to the advance slot being used.

> Advance slot high compression and low compression
> engines—15L
> Advance slot GT engines—10L

4.49 Ignition Timing

Once the ignition timing has been set it cannot alter to any great extent unless the fixing at the base of the distributor becomes loose. Once the distributor is released the timing is lost and the engine must be re-timed. To re-time the ignition proceed as explained below:

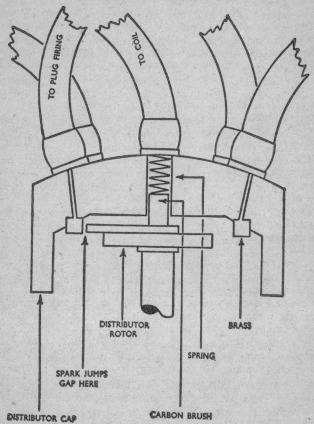

Fig. 23. The path of the current through the distributor, to the plugs. A spring strip on the rotor may replace the brush.

(1) Adjust the contact breaker points. (See 4.45, p. 89.)
(2) Remove the sparking plugs to make the engine easy to turn. Turn the engine clockwise until No. 1 piston

is rising on the compression stroke. No. 1 piston is the one nearest the radiator. The compression stroke may be identified by lightly closing the plug opening in No. 1 cylinder with the thumb while the engine is turned in a clockwise direction. Pressure on the thumb and/or escape of air will indicate that the piston is rising on the compression stroke.

The engine may be turned by pulling on the fan belt. *Do not turn the engine by turning the fan.*

(3)   When timing the engine it is necessary to know when the contact breaker points have opened. A precise way of doing this is to connect the test lamp, fitted with a low wattage bulb, between the two low tension terminals on the ignition coil. If the engine is turned when the ignition is switched on, the light will go *on* when the points *close* and go *out* when the points open.

(4)   Having determined that the piston is rising on the compression stroke, align the timing marks on the timing cover with the 'nick' in the crankshaft pulley rim. See Fig. 24 and 10.12, p. 149.

(5)   With the distributor clamp bolt released to enable the distributor to be turned and the test lamp fitted as described in (3) above: remove the distributor cap and turn the distributor clockwise until the test lamp lights. Now very slowly turn the distributor anticlockwise and stop turning immediately the lamp goes out. Carefully hold the distributor so that it cannot move *and tighten the clamp bolt.* Do not overtighten the bolt. The rotor brass should now be opposite No. 1 pick-up brass inside the distributor cap. That is the one to which the lead to No. 1 plug is connected. For the order in which the plug leads are connected please refer to Fig. 21.

(6)   Check the adjustment on the road. With the engine at normal operating temperature, accelerate quickly (wide throttle opening) from 20 m.p.h. (32 k.p.h.) to 40 m.p.h. (64 k.p.h.) in *top* gear. If there is heavy pinking during acceleration the ignition is too far advanced. Retard the ignition slightly by slackening the clamp bolt at the base of the distributor and turning the distributor *very slightly* in an anti-clockwise direction and re-tightening the distributor clamp bolt. Again check

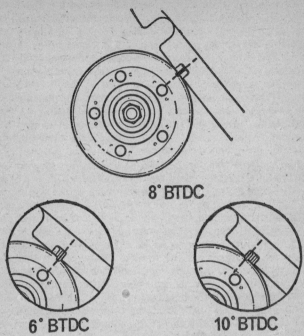

Fig. 24. Ignition timing marks.

the adjustment by repeating the road test. The ignition timing is correct when, while making the acceleration test, there is just a trace of pinking. Adjustment and road testing should be continued on a trial and error basis until the correct setting is obtained.

4.50 Ignition Timing Marks
The ignition timing marks are on the crankshaft pulley and timing case cover. Fig 24 shows the different combinations of the marks to give different ignition timing settings. 10.12, page 149 shows which timing mark to use for each model.

4.51 The Horn
If the horn fails to sound when the push is depressed and the ignition is switched 'On' this would indicate a fault in the horn wiring or in the horn itself.

Place the ear close to the horn while the push is depressed and released several times in rapid succession. Even a horn that is faulty will usually emit some sound. If some sound is heard, this would, on the face of it, indicate a fault in the horn. To prove if this is the case detach the wires connected to the horn and remove the horn from the car. Connect a short length of wire to one of the horn terminals and while holding the other end of this wire in contact with either of the battery terminals, press the horn terminal with no wire attached to it on to the other battery terminal. The horn will now sound normally, if it is in order. If it does not sound it is faulty and should be renewed.

Assuming that no sound could be heard when the first test was made, disconnect both the wires connected to the horn. Connect one of the test lamp wires to each of the horn wires and, with the ignition switched 'On' depress the horn push. The test lamp should light, indicating that the horn circuit is in order. If the test lamp does not light when this test is made, connect the purple/black wire via the test lamp to some good earth point. The test lamp should light when the push is depressed, if it does not, faulty wiring or push is indicated. If the lamp lights, again connect the two horn wires with the test lamp. If the lamp fails to light there is a faulty horn earth. In this case either a new horn earth point should be provided or the old earth wire connection should be removed, cleaned and replaced.

4.52 Fuses

The fuse box is fitted to the engine rear bulkhead. Early Escorts had six fused circuits, later models seven fused circuits. In both types of fuse box the fuses are numbered to enable the fuse and the circuit it protects to be identified. All the fuses are rated at 8 amps. Only 8 amp fuses must be used, if fuse renewal becomes necessary.

On examining the fuses it will be observed that some fuse positions are vacant (no fuses fitted). These fuse positions are provided as feed points for accessories. The seven fuse box has positions 1, 6 and 7 vacant. Fuse point 1 is a feed direct from the battery, points 1 and 6 are connected to the output side of the ignition switch, so that any accessory connected to these points would only operate when the ignition

switch was in the 'On' position. The following keys detail
the work of the various fuses:

Key to 6 fuse block
1. RH main beam
2. LH main beam
3. RH dipped beam
4. LH dipped beam
5. RH side and tail lamps
6. LH side and tail lamps

Key to 7 fuse block
1. Interior lamp and cigar lighter
2. LH side and tail lamp, number plate lamp
3. RH side and tail lamp, panel illumination
4. Main beam
5. Dipped beam
6. Direction indicators, stop lamps, heater motor
7. Windscreen wiper motor.

4.53 The Alternator
Alternators were not fitted to the early Escorts.

Faults: First check that the battery connections are clean
and tight and that the drive belt is correctly adjusted. Because
of the way it is connected, the ignition warning light provides
a guide to diagnose an alternator fault. The light should always
be on when the ignition is switched on and the engine is
stopped. It should go out when the engine starts and remain
out all the time the engine is running. Any variation from this
sequence, going on and out at different engine speeds or if the
light brightens and dims at different engine speeds, almost
certainly indicates an alternator fault. If the ignition warning
light fails to come on at all, check the bulb. If the bulb is
sound, a faulty alternator is indicated.

If the battery is even momentarily connected the 'wrong
way round', the alternator rectifying system will be damaged.
DO NOT disconnect the battery when the engine is running.

5
Clutch and Transmission

5.1 General

The drive is via a single plate dry clutch with diaphragm spring and four speed gearbox, the mainshaft of which is connected to the rear axle differential by a propellor shaft with a universal joint at each end.

The clutch is cable operated.

The gearbox is of the constant mesh helical gear type with syncromesh on all four forward speeds. On certain models automatic transmission is fitted. The gear change lever is of the floor type.

5.2 Automatic Transmission (See also 5.3 below)

The transmission consists of a three speed epicyclic gearbox and torque converter, gear selection being effected by brake bands and clutches, which are hydraulically operated. Fluid under pressure, to operate the system, is obtained from a gear type pump.

The control is a T handle, floor mounted between the two front seats. The lever moves in a gate which is marked with the various gear positions. The lever is moved until it is opposite the gear position required and the symbol in that position is illuminated when the side lamps are switched on. The gear positions are marked:

P R N D 2 1

The engine can only be started when P or N is selected.

P PARK – The transmission is locked in this position and it should be used in conjunction with the handbrake when parking. DO NOT select P when the car is moving.

R REVERSE – Select R to reverse. DO NOT select R when the car is moving.

N NEUTRAL – The transmission is disconnected.

D DRIVE – All forward gear changes are made automatically.

2 DRIVE in 1 and 2 – Automatic gear changes between 1st and 2nd gears. When 2 is selected an immediate change is made into 2nd gear. Therefore DO NOT select 2 unless the road speed is suitable, not much in excess of 55 m.p.h.

1 LOCK 1st gear locked in. When 1 is selected, 1st gear will immediately be engaged unless the road speed is too high, in which case 1st gear does not engage until the speed has dropped sufficiently. Once selected, 1st gear is held until the control lever is moved.

Earlier cars had a steering column mounted selection lever and instead of positions 2 and 1, only an L position is provided. 1st gear will be lock held if L is selected below 5 m.p.h. If selected from a higher speed (which should only be within the safe range of 2nd gear) 2nd will be engaged and held locked unless speed drops below 5 m.p.h. when the transmission would go into 1st lock. The lock holds thus provided enable engine braking to be obtained when required for long descents. Their overiding action continues until D is reselected.

5.3 Notes on the Automatic Transmission

The car cannot be push or tow started. The car may be towed in N at speeds below 30 m.p.h. (48 k.p.h.) for up to a distance of 15 miles, provided the transmission is not faulty. Otherwise the propellor shaft must be removed before the car is towed.

For reasons of safety, the button on the right-hand side of the T handle (left-hand side for left-hand drive cars) must be held pressed when making these selections:

P to R	2 to 1
R to P	N to R
D to 2	

When the accelerator pedal is depressed, there is a point of increased resistance at the 'full throttle' position. Beyond this point, is the 'kick down' position. If the pedal is depressed beyond this point when starting from rest, maximum acceleration through all the gears will be obtained.

If 'kick down' is used when the car is travelling at 25–30 m.p.h. in 3rd (top) gear, 2nd gear will select, if used when the car speed is below 25 m.p.h., 1st gear will select. The gears are held so long as the 'kick down' position is retained. The

D

effect gives full power acceleration when required, as when overtaking.

Do not increase engine r.p.m. above tickover speed when the car is stationary. The car will tend to move forward when DRIVE is selected. The brakes should be applied to hold the car stationary when necessary.

5.4 Fault Symptoms, Clutch
  (1) **The clutch slips.**
  (2) **The clutch drags.**
  (3) **The clutch will not engage.**
  (4) **The clutch will not disengage.**
  (5) **Drive through clutch varies—judder.**
  (6) **Clutch fierce.**

5.5 Causes and Cures
(1) When the clutch slips the engine speed rises without a corresponding increase in the speed of the car. Of course the clutch normally slips during the act of engagement, but there should be none once the clutch is engaged. If slip occurs when the clutch is fully engaged very rapid wear of the friction linings will take place.

As the clutch friction linings wear, the free movement of the release arm is gradually reduced and in time the clutch will be partially held out of engagement by the release mechanism. This will lead to rapid wear of the linings. As soon as any signs of slip appear the cable adjustment should be checked and corrected if necessary. See 5.6 below.

Other causes of clutch slip are oil on the clutch linings or a fault in the diaphragm spring. Excessively worn clutch linings may have the same effect. The operating cable may be seized in the outer casing.

(2) The effect of drag is that the clutch will not completely free the drive ; with the engine running and a gear engaged the car moves forward even when the clutch pedal is fully depressed. Cable adjustment is required at intervals to allow for wear of the friction linings. Failure to maintain the correct adjustment results in the clutch pedal having too much free movement.

(3) See (1) above.

(4) See (2) above.

(5) Judder is a 'Jerky' action as the clutch is engaged. It may

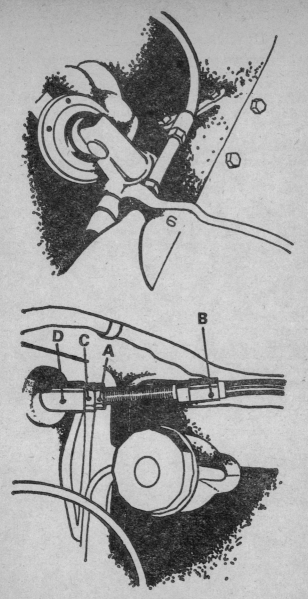

Fig. 25. Clutch adjustment. How the clutch cable is attached to the clutch pedal.

be oil or grease on the clutch linings, or loose or worn engine mountings. It may also be due to a broken diaphragm spring. The clutch friction plate may be distorted.

(6) A fierce clutch takes up the drive suddenly even when it is very carefully engaged, so that a smooth start is difficult or impossible. It may be due to excessive wear of the friction linings. The engine mountings may be worn or loose. The shaft and/or clutch disc splines may be worn. A distorted pressure plate will cause the trouble.

5.6 Clutch Cable Adjustment and How to Fit a New Cable

Refer to Fig. 25.

(1) Slacken locknut A on clutch cable adjuster B.

(2) With the clutch pedal *pulled* up against its stop and the cable adjuster pulled back, the distance between the adjusting nut C and its abutment D should be between 0·138–0·144 in. (3·5–3·7 mm).

(3) If this clearance is not present, turn the adjusting nut until the correct clearance is obtained then, using two spanners, tighten the locknut against the adjusting nut. Re-check that the setting is correct.

(4) With the cable correctly adjusted, as explained above, there should be ½ to ¾ inch (12–19 mm) free movement in the clutch pedal.

(5) There should be no free movement in the clutch release arm. Play at this point would indicate a fault.

Note that on early Escorts the clutch adjuster abuts against the engine bulkhead while on later models there is an abutment extension on the clutch housing. The two positions are shown in Fig. 25.

How to Fit a New Clutch Cable

The front of the car must be raised clear of the ground to give access to the underside. Preferably use a pit or ramps. If the front of the car is jacked up fit stands or other *secure supports*. Do *not* get under the car when it is supported only on the jack or jacks.

(1) Slacken the cable adjuster locknut (see note 5.6 above) and turn both adjuster nut and locknut well up the adjuster stem (see Fig. 25) to slacken the cable.

(2) Remove the clip from the top of the clutch pedal (see Fig. 26). Twist the attachment pin, withdraw it through the slot in the pedal end and pull the cable through

the bulkhead, towards the engine.

(3) Pull back the rubber cover over the clutch operating rod on the clutch housing and detach the end of the cable from the lever.

Fitting the New Cable

The cable is fitted by reversing the removal procedure. Pass the correct end of the cable through the engine bulkhead,

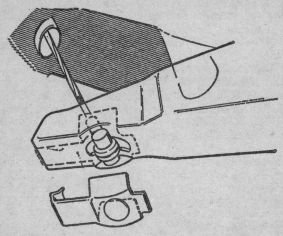

Fig. 26. Fitting the clutch cable to the clutch operating arm.

grease the attachment pin, fit it to the pedal and replace the clip.

Fit the opposite end of the cable to the clutch release lever and adjust the cable as explained above.

5.7 Propellor Shaft Removal

Some Escorts have a one piece shaft with a universal joint at each end while others have a two piece shaft with three universal joints. To remove a shaft proceed thus:

(1) Mark the connecting flanges across the joints so that they can be re-assembled as they were originally and so preserve the dynamic balance of the assembly.

(2) Remove the flange nuts and bolts and lower the rear end of the shaft sufficiently to allow it to be withdrawn

from the gearbox. This applies to the one piece shaft only. In the case of the two piece shaft the shaft cannot be withdrawn from the gearbox until the support bracket for the mid-bearing is detached by removal of the two fixing bolts.

Notes On Re-fitting the Propellor Shaft: Slide the front end of the shaft into the gearbox, turning it a little to engage the splines. Be very careful not to damage the oil seal in the housing or to cause damage to the gearing. With the front end of the shaft in position, lift the rear end and re-connect the flanges after aligning the marks made earlier. Tighten the nuts to a torque of 15–18 lb. ft. (2·1–2·4 kg.m).

In the case of the two piece shaft, after inserting the front end of the shaft, re-fit the mid-bearing support, leaving the nuts loose at this stage. Lift the rear end of the shaft and connect it, following the instructions given above. When the two ends of the shaft are secured tighten the mid bearing support bracket bolt nuts to a torque of 15–18 lb. ft. (2·1–2·4 kg.m).

Some oil may escape from the gearbox when the shaft is removed and therefore the level in the gearbox should be checked after the shaft has been re-fitted, and topped up as required.

5.8 Renewing a Universal Joint

(1) Remove the circlips. This is most easily done with a pair of circlip pliers (see Fig. 27). If the bearing yoke is then tapped with a soft faced hammer the bearing cups can be displaced from it.

(2) Take all the old parts of the joint and place them so that they cannot become mixed with the parts of the new joint that is to be fitted.

(3) Fit the new oil seals to the seal retainers and locate them on the spiders and up against the shoulders. The oil seals must face the bearing cups to be fitted. Place the spider in the drive shaft yoke and assemble the needle rollers in the bearing cups, retaining them in position with lithium base grease—packing the cup but leaving a little space for expansion of the grease when it becomes warm. Care and patience is required to re-assemble the joint.

(4) With the bearing cups fitted to one yoke, re-fit the cir-

clips. Re-assemble the two remaining bearings in the same way.

5.9 Transmission Fault Symptoms

(1) Transmission noisy.
(2) Vibration in transmission.
(3) Gears jump out of engagement.
(4) Gears are difficult to engage.
(5) Gears will not disengage.
(6) No drive to wheels, gear and clutch engaged.

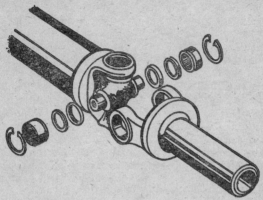

Fig. 27. A universal joint. Some Escorts have two of these and some three in the propellor shaft.

5.10 Causes and Cures

(1) Transmission whine is usually due to general wear. Bearing wear gives rise to incorrect meshing of the gear teeth and excessive end play develops. It may be due to faulty bearings and/or broken gear teeth. Check that the oil level is correct.

Whine in the differential is also likely to be due to the faults mentioned above. Knocks may be due to broken gear teeth.

(2) This may be a bent propellor shaft or loose flange or universal joints. The knock, if due to these causes, will not be present when the car is stationary with the engine running. However a knock that is only present when the car is on the move may be due to a loose wheel.

103

(3) May be due to broken or weak spring behind the selector rod locating steel ball. It may be due to a worn groove in the selector rod or the selector fork may be loose.

(4) This may be due to faulty syncromesh mechanism or to incorrect adjustment of the clutch (see 5.6 above). May be due to a seized gear lever ball joint. Check the gearbox oil level.

(5) May be due to jammed selector shafts or to a fault in the syncromesh cones. It may be due to faulty clutch adjustment, see above.

(6) Partial loss of drive may be due to failure of the clutch to engage properly caused by extreme wear of the friction linings or incorrect adjustment, see 5.6 above.

5.11 Topping-up the Automatic Transmission

The car should be on a level surface and the transmission unit should be at normal operating temperature. This temperature should be reached after a minimum of 5 miles driving. Select P and allow the engine to idle for two minutes. With the engine still idling in P withdraw the dipstick and wipe it with a piece of clean fluffless cloth. The dipstick is located in a tube at the right hand side at the rear of the engine compartment. Re-insert the dipstick with the engine still running and immediately withdraw it. If necessary add transmission fluid to bring the level up to the 'Full' mark on the dipstick.

If it should be necessary to check the fluid level when the engine is cold, proceed as explained above. The correct level is then $\frac{3}{8}$ in. below the 'Full' mark on the dipstick. The level should be re-checked as soon as the unit has reached normal operating temperature. The fluid is not drained from the gearbox, topping up maintenance only being required.

The transmission is cooled by air flow over it. Therefore the underside of the unit must be maintained free from mud. This applies also to the stone guards and ventilator grilles. If this is not done overheating may occur.

5.12 Topping-up the Rear Axle

A square headed level/filler plug is located on the rear axle casing, facing to the rear. To top-up remove the plug after removing dirt from and immediately around it and add approved oil until it runs out of the plug opening. Securely replace the plug.

6

Suspension

6.1 General

Shock absorber/spring units are used as the suspension ele-
ments for each front wheel as shown in Fig. 28. Each unit
consists of a hydraulic telescopic shock absorber round which
is placed a coiled spring, located between a seat on the top
sliding section of the shock absorber and a second seat on
the lower shock absorber member, compression of the shock
absorber resulting in compression of the coil spring.

An upward stop to wheel travel is imposed by a bump rubber fitted at the top of the suspension unit. On early Escorts
upward travel of the wheel was limited by closure of the
spring coils.

Downward wheel movement is restricted by a stop, either
at the bottom of the suspension unit or in the shock
absorber.

Each front wheel is positioned laterally by a track control
arm connected between the bottom of the suspension unit and
the chassis, rubber bushed joints permitting vertical movement of the outer end of the arm and attached spring unit.
Fore-and-aft movement is controlled by a stabiliser bar. This
is a U shaped bar extending across the 'axle' in front, each
end of the bar being flexibly connected to the track control
rod near its outer end, see Fig. 29. The centre run of the bar
is held in rubber bushed brackets attached to the body. On
some Escorts the stabiliser bar is replaced by two compression struts, one to each wheel as shown by Fig. 30. The compression strut connects between an anchor point on the track
control arm and a rubber mounting on a chassis bracket. Due
to the rubber mounting, the strut will compress slightly under
load and thus permit slight fore-and-aft movement of the
wheels in order to damp down peak shock loads which would
otherwise be transmitted to the steering linkage.

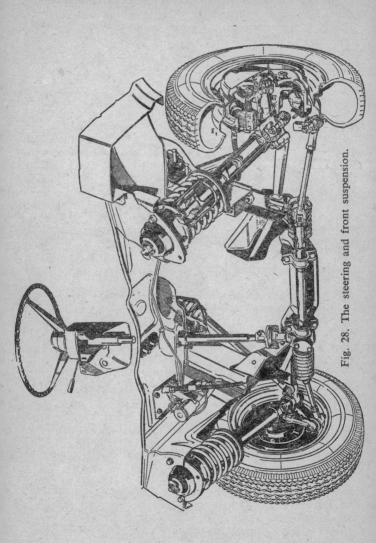

Fig. 28. The steering and front suspension.

The rear suspension system incorporates conventional semi-elliptical leaf type springs. The axle attachment point of the springs is displaced from the spring centre towards the front

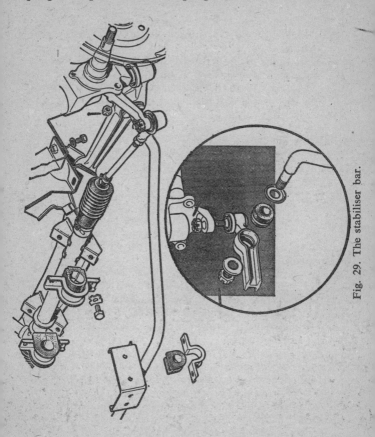

Fig. 29. The stabiliser bar.

end of the spring. The shortening of the springs at these points reduces spring distortion caused by torque reaction.

The spring action is damped by two telescopic hydraulic shock absorbers, one to each side, connected between a reinforced attachment point on the body floor and another point on the rear axle.

On both front and rear suspension rubber is interposed at all body attachment points to reduce the transmission of road noise and vibration to the body.

6.2 Fault Symptoms

(1) **Heavy road shocks transmitted to body—suspension bottoms.**

(2) **Suspension lively—excessive bounce on rough roads.**

(3) **Car leans to one side.**

(4) **Knocking noises from suspension, particularly when driving over rough surfaces.**

(5) **Suspension rattles.**

6.3 Causes and Cures

(1) Shock absorbers faulty. See (3) below and 6.4.

(2) Shock absorbers faulty. See (3) below and 6.4.

(3) Tired or broken springs. Examine the front suspension units for broken and/or closed coils. Examine the rear springs for broken leaves. Fitting a new spring or new front suspension unit requires special tools and the reader is warned that it is dangerous to attempt repairs to the front suspension units without these tools. For information on rear spring repairs see 6.5 below.

(4) May be due to worn shock absorber rubber bushes. The shock absorber mountings may be loose. The track control arm rubber bushes may be worn. The rear spring forward mounting rubber bushes and rear shackle bushes may be worn. Check the rear spring U bolts for tightness.

(5) The front suspension stabiliser bar may be loose. Check that it is tight in both track control rods, particularly the end where the rubber bush is fitted. Check that the bar is tight in its mounting clamps. Where compression struts are fitted in place of the stabiliser bar, check that each strut is properly secured and that the rubber buffers incorporated in the rear attachment point of the struts are sound. Check both front suspension units for springs with broken coils and the tightness of all attachment fittings.

Check the rear spring U bolts for tightness and inspect the rear springs for leaf breakage.

6.4 Removal of Rear Shock Absorbers

The rear shock absorbers are connected between a bracket

retained in position by the spring U bolts and a body cross member. The nuts may prove to be very tight, due to the effects of water. It is worth while applying penetrating oil to the nuts some time before work is commenced. Use a ring spanner. If the nuts have been damaged it may be necessary to cut the bolts with a hacksaw, in which case you should have new bolts ready. Your best means of access to underneath the car is by a pit. Ramps may be used. If the car is jacked up very secure supports must be used. Do not get under the car when it is supported on a jack or jacks. If the rear of the car is lifted the front wheels must be securely chocked first.

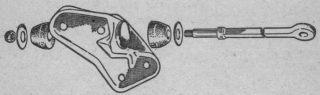

Fig. 30. The compression strut. On some Escorts two compression struts will be found to be fitted instead of a stabiliser bar.

Unscrew the nuts holding the shock absorber in position and pull the unit clear.

To fit a replacement shock absorber or replace the old unit, place it on the fixing bolts and fit the nuts. There is a washer under the bottom nut. The nuts are self locking and therefore only one is fitted to each bolt. Screw up the nuts until ready to tighten, but do not tighten. The weight of the car *must be on the wheels on level ground when the bolts are tightened.* If the bolts are tightened when the weight of the car is off the wheels the rubber bushes will have a very short life. For the correct tightening torque, see 10.8, p. 148.

6.5 Rear Spring Removal and Re-fitting
While removing and re-fitting a rear spring is not a very difficult task and could be carried out by many owners, lack of equipment does present some difficulty. See Fig. 31.

(1) Securely chock both front wheels. The rear of the car must be lifted clear of the ground to provide ample working space and it must be held safe and secure on strong supports—not just on jacks.

(2) It is necessary to support the axle. This can be done with wood blocks using a jack to lift the axle as required. The problem of positioning the axle is more acute when re-fitting the spring. Detach the shock absorber from its bottom attachment point.

(3) Remove the shackle nuts from the links at the rear of the spring and pull the two plates clear.

(4) Remove the two rubbers from the body fixing point.

(5) Remove the nut, spring washer and bolt from the spring front attachment point.

(6) Remove the U bolts, and hence lift clear the plate and bump stop on the top of the axle.

(7) Remove the rubber block and its support plate and, finally the spring assembly.

(8) Cut one of the flanges of the rear spring eye rubber and remove the rubber bush from the spring eye. See notes on re-fitting the spring assembly below.

To Re-fit a Spring Assembly proceed thus:

(1) Fit a new rear spring eye rubber bush. The bush is flanged with a triangular centre section. When fitted, one of the three corners must face downwards. Concerning the fitting of the bushes, see the note at the end of this chapter.

(2) Fit a new rubber bush unit to the front spring eye. Position the front spring eye in its attachment bracket and fit the bolt and nut. Screw the nut up finger tight only.

(3) Fit the rubber insulator block on the spring with support plate on top of the block.

(4) Fit the bump stop and two U bolts. Fit the U bolt plate and nuts. Partially tighten the nuts (5 lb. ft.). Fit the two half bushes to the rear spring attachment point.

(5) Position the spring to allow the shackle plate/bolt assemblies to be fitted and when they are in position fit the nuts and screw up finger tight only. Re-fit the bottom end of the shock absorber.

(6) Lower the car so that its weight is on the wheels.

(7) Tighten the spring rear shackle nuts, the front attachment bolt, the U bolt nuts and the bottom shock

110

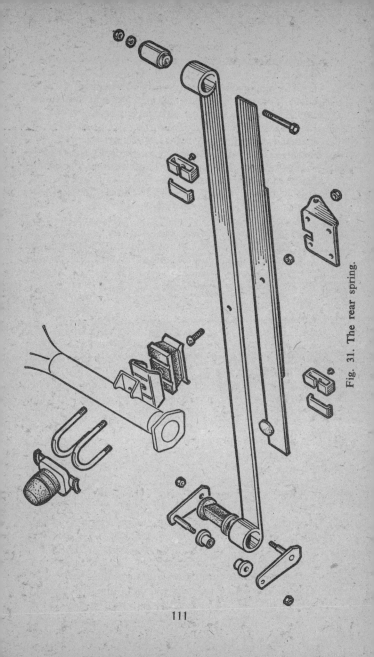

Fig. 31. The rear spring.

absorber fixing to the torque ratings given in 10.8, p. 148.

Notes on Fitting the Spring: It is most important that the U bolt nuts, the spring front attachment bolt and the spring rear shackle bolts should not be tightened until the weight of the car is on the wheels.

Difficulties arise in fitting the front spring eye bush and the rear spring eye bush but the possession of special tools P5029, P5029-5 and CP5029-A makes the work simple. Without these tools the operator must devise his own tools. Given the necessary ingenuity the work can be done using a bolt or a length of screwed rod and some nuts plus short lengths of different diameter steel tubing and strong washers. While no special care need be taken when extracting the old bushes, special care is needed when fitting the new bushes or they may be damaged and an unsatisfactory repair will result.

7

The Braking System

7.1 General

The brakes on all four wheels on all models are hydraulically operated. The parking brake operates on the rear wheels only, connection between the brakes and the handbrake lever being by cables and a mechanical linkage. The lever is of the 'pull up' type, located between the front seats.

On some models disc brakes are fitted to the front wheels and a servo assistance unit may also be fitted, otherwise the front brakes are of the two leading shoe type. The vacuum servo unit works off the engine induction system and is fitted as standard to the GT model, the Sport and the 1300 Estate, and is an optional extra on the other models. When servo is fitted the hydraulic master cylinder is mounted on the servo unit. The unit consists essentially of an airtight chamber divided by a diaphragm. Both sides of the divided chamber are in communication with the induction system when the brakes are off. Thus when the engine is running and the brakes are off both sides of the chamber are subjected to an equal vacuum effect and therefore no movement of the diaphragm takes place.

Depressing the brake pedal applies the brakes in the normal manner, the pedal moving the piston in the master cylinder by a connecting rod linkage. However this movement also causes air to be admitted to the rear part of the chamber, atmospheric pressure therefore causes the diaphragm to move forward. This movement and the force behind it is communicated to the master cylinder operating rod and so augments the pressure of the driver's foot on the brake pedal. When the brake pedal is released the effect is to again equalise the degree of vacuum on both sides of the diaphragm so that no operating force is produced.

The servo unit is designed to provide a differential effect; the pressure difference created between the two sides of the

113

diaphragm depending on how far the brake pedal is depressed; full pressure and therefore applying force from the unit, is only obtained when the brake pedal is fully depressed.

7.2 Fault Symptoms

  (1) **Brakes lack stopping power.**
  (2) **Excessive pedal pressure is required.**
  (3) **Pedal travel too great.**
  (4) **Brake pedal needs to be 'pumped' to apply the brakes.**
  (5) **Car pulls to one side when the brakes are applied.**
  (6) **Brakes 'grab'.**
  (7) **Brakes 'squeal'.**
  (8) **Brake pedal has a 'spongy' feel.**
  (9) **Handbrake is ineffective.**
  (10) **Brakes bind.**
  (11) **Braking system warning light 'On'.**

7.3 Causes and Cures

(1) Brakes Lack Stopping Power: This is usually caused by brake lining wear, the remedy being to fit new shoes, if adjustment fails to cure the trouble. In the case of front disc brakes new brake pads may be required. The trouble may be caused if oil or grease gets on to the brake linings or pads perhaps when the car is being serviced. A similar effect is present if brake fluid gets on to the linings. This could be due to a faulty seal and would be obvious by the loss of fluid. The servo unit may be faulty.

(2) This is normally due to the same causes as those listed in (1) above.

(3) If the brakes are of the manually adjustable type (see 7.4 below) adjustment of the shoes may be all that is required to restore normal pedal movement. Air in the hydraulic system will result in excessive pedal travel, see 7.9 and 7.10, p. 119 and p. 121. A leak in the system will have the same effect.

(4) This is due to air in the hydraulic system or excessive shoe movement due to incorrect adjustment, see 7.9 and 7.10, pp. 119 and 121, and 7.4 below.

(5) Braking effect greater one side than the other, is due to unbalanced brakes. If the car pulls to the right the weak brakes are on the left. If the car pulls to the left the weak brakes are on the right. The possible causes are incorrectly

adjusted brakes, worn through linings, oiled linings, loose brake back plate, scored or distorted drums or discs. It may also be caused by the fitting of linings of the incorrect grade.

Check that the handbrake releases completely when the lever is in the 'off' position. If the symptom is accompanied by 'grab' see (6) below. One or more of the brake drums may be cracked. It may be a suspension fault, see chapter 6.

(6) The brakes 'grab' when light pressure on the brake pedal causes the brakes to come hard on, so that progressive braking is impossible. The fault may be caused by distorted or scored brake drums or discs. The brake backplate may be loose (drum brakes). Check also for loose hub bearings, rear spring loose or loose front suspension.

(7) A fault sometimes difficult to remedy. Remove the drum and clean free from lining dust. Remove the dust also from backplate and shoes, but take care not to get any grease or oil on the shoe linings. To cure front brake (disc brake) squeal, try fitting new pads.

(8) Usually due to air in the system; if it is it can be cured by bleeding the system, see 7.9 and 7.10, pp. 119, 121. Check the master cylinder for tightness on its mountings. There may be a cracked brake drum. The master cylinder may be worn. New linings sometimes cause this effect until 'bedded-in'. There may be leakage of fluid from the system.

(9) May be caused by the brake shoes being in need of adjustment. If the handbrake becomes ineffective a possible cause would be stretch in the handbrake cable, see 7.7, 7.8 below.

(10) Check that the affected brake is correctly adjusted. Overadjustment will cause the shoes to bind. Check that the handbrake is releasing completely when the brake lever is returned to the fully off position. Remove the brake drum from the wheel where the fault is present and check that the shoe pull-off springs are not broken, strained or incorrectly fitted. Have an assistant very carefully depress the brake pedal by a *small* amount and then release it. Observe if the shoes return promptly and fully to the off position when the pedal is released. *Warning:* The greatest care is needed when making this test or the piston (or pistons, where there are two) will be pushed out of the wheel cylinders. The pedal should be depressed by only a very small amount, just sufficient for movement to be observed. If the shoes are sticking it may be due to the pistons(s) being jammed in the cylinder(s).

Check that the shoes are free to move on their pivots.

The fault may be due to swollen cups in the master cylinder or wheel cylinder(s). This would be caused by contaminated brake fluid, often caused by using a container contaminated with oil to top up the system. The by-pass port in the master cylinder may be obstructed. If the hydraulic cups are faulty, drain the system by pumping all the fluid out through the bleed nipples (see 7.9 and 7.10, pp. 119, 121), then wash out with methylated spirits. Renew all seals in the system, refill with approved brake fluid and then bleed the system.

(11) Fault in one of the brake lines. Differential valve not centralised. See 7.10.

7.4 Brake adjustment

Disc brakes are fitted to the front wheels of some Escorts; these are the Sport, the GT and the 1300 Estate car. The 8 cwt. vans are also fitted with disc brakes. They are self adjusting.

When drum brakes are fitted to the front wheels these are of the two leading shoe type, each shoe having its own operating cylinder and adjuster. Two square ended adjusters will be found on each front wheel backplate. To adjust these brakes:

(1) Apply the handbrake.
(2) Jack up the front wheel on which the brakes are to be adjusted, until it is clear of the ground. Turn the wheel and note if it is quite free. It ought to be free, but if not back off both adjusters by turning them anti-clockwise. This should free the wheel.
(3) Turn one adjuster clockwise until the wheel is locked, then back the adjuster off just sufficiently to allow the wheel to turn freely. Repeat this procedure for the other adjuster. The brake is then correctly adjusted.
(4) Repeat the method of adjustment on the other front wheel.

Rear Brake Adjustment: The rear brakes are of the leading/trailing shoe drum type with one adjuster on the brake backplate. See Fig. 34, p. 122. To adjust these brakes:

(1) Securely chock the front wheels, then fully release the handbrake.
(2) Jack up the rear wheel on which the brakes are to be

adjusted until it is clear of the ground. Check that the wheel turns freely, if it does not make sure the handbrake is fully off. If the handbrake is proved to be fully off, there is a fault in the brake and the drum should be removed so that the shoes can be inspected and the cause of the binding discovered.

(3) Assuming that the wheel rotates freely, turn the square ended adjuster clockwise until the wheel is locked, then back the adjuster off just sufficiently to allow the wheel to turn freely. The brake is then correctly adjusted.

(4) Repeat the above procedure on the other rear wheel.

7.5 Notes on Brake Adjustment

When new shoes have been fitted the linings bed down very rapidly over the first 50–100 miles (80–160 km) and it is therefore essential to check and adjust the brakes once or twice during this period. Brakes should be adjusted when the drums are cold. When the brakes are properly adjusted there should be negligible rubbing. Brakes that bind will result in the generation of considerable heat and this will cause reduced braking efficiency and may vaporise the brake fluid. Another result will be waste of fuel.

7.6 Checking Disc Brakes for Wear

Because no adjustment is required the need to check the brake pads for wear should not be forgotten. Pads must be renewed when excessively worn. If this is not done the linings will wear through and the metal backing will come into contact with the brake disc. This will cause damage that cannot be remedied simply by fitting new pads. The linings should be inspected every 6000 miles (9000 km). Pads must be renewed when the lining is down to 1/16 in. thick (1·5 mm) thick. If the pads are not renewed when close to the wear limit they should be inspected more frequently. The pads may be inspected without removing them from the caliper assembly. The best way to check the pads is to remove the wheel and inspect them in the light from a torch or inspection lamp. Disc brake pad renewal is dealt with in 7.12, p. 128.

7.7 Handbrake adjustment

The correct handbrake adjustment is normally obtained when the rear brakes are adjusted. Therefore if the handbrake lever movement is excessive, it probably indicates that the rear brakes need to be adjusted.

It is not usually necessary to adjust the handbrake cables, but in the course of time such adjustment may become necessary.

To adjust the handbrake mechanism

(1) Securely chock the front wheels and make sure the handbrake lever is fully in the 'Off' position.

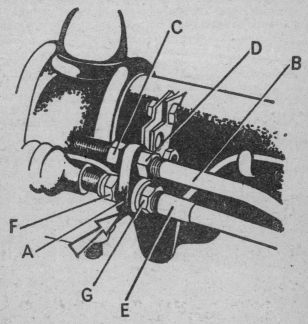

Fig. 32. The handbrake adjustment.

(2) Jack up the rear of the car and lower it on to secure supports.

(3) The equalising bracket is fitted on the rear axle near the nearside wheel. Turn the brake adjuster on this wheel clockwise until there is a feeling of slight drag when the wheel is turned.

(4) The equaliser bracket A Fig. 32 should be either at

118

right angles to the rear axle or offset towards the centre-line of the car by ⅛ in. (3 mm). If not within these limits adjust the length of the transverse rod B until the bracket is within the stated limits. To lengthen the rod, release locknut C and turn nut D towards the wheel. To shorten the rod, release nut D and turn nut C towards the base of the threaded portion on the rod (away from the wheel). Both nuts must be tight when the adjustment of the rod is complete. If the adjustment of the effective length of the rod is too great so that the equalising bracket is moved too much in the direction of the car centreline the brakes will bind when the handbrake lever is in the 'Off' position.

(5) If any slack exists in the handbrake cable remove it by extending the cable adjuster E. To extend the adjuster, release locknut F and turn it back a little on its threads. Turn nut G to move it in the direction of the wheel. When all slack from the inner cable has been removed tighten nut F.

(6) Now turn back the wheel brake adjuster (anti-clockwise) two or three clicks. Check that the wheel is free to rotate. If there is some rubbing slack off the wheel adjuster one more click. If the wheel is still not quite free the whole adjusting procedure must be repeated.

7.8 Notes on Handbrake Adjustment

When working on the brakes, look for obvious faults. It is important that you should work in good light so as to see clearly. Before making any adjustments have an assistant apply and release the handbrake several times while you watch from underneath the car. Note if the brakes move promptly to the 'Off' position when the lever is released. Check that the cables are in good condition. After long service it is worth removing the old clevis pins and fitting new ones. Grooves wear in the pins and this gives rise to excessive movement in the system. While under the car look also for leakage from the footbrake pipes and connections. Handbrake layout is shown by Fig. 35, p. 125.

7.9 Bleeding the Brakes (Single Line)

(1) First check the fluid level in the master cylinder reservoir. The reservoir is located at the rear of the brake

pedal pivot (or on top of the servo unit if fitted). Clean the cap before removing to prevent dirt entering the system. Top up with fluid if necessary; it is essential that the fluid level in the reservoir is maintained because the level lowers as the bleeding process proceeds. If the level falls too low, air will be drawn into the system and the bleeding process will be rendered abortive. Therefore watch the level carefully as bleeding proceeds and add *fresh* fluid as required.

(2) It is necessary to have a brake bleeding tube (obtainable from any accessory store) and a small, clear, container such as a glass jam jar. Remove the rubber dust cover from the right hand front wheel bleed nipple and fit the end of the bleed tube to the nipple. The nipple will be on the caliper unit if disc brakes are fitted or on the backplate if drum brakes are fitted.

(3) Place the other end of the bleed tube in the clear container so that it is touching the bottom and pour in sufficient brake fluid to submerge the end of the tube. Slacken the bleed nipple, using a spanner, by half a turn.

(4) Have an assistant observe the container while the brake pedal is slowly depressed. This will pump fluid from the system into the container and any air in the system will be carried into the fluid in the container as air bubbles. The pedal should be depressed and then allowed to return unassisted. Wait 2-3 seconds before again depressing the pedal. When continuing the pumping action fails to pump out any more air bubbles, hold the pedal in the depressed position while the bleed nipple is tightened. Do not over tighten the nipple. Replace the rubber dust cover on the nipple.

(5) Repeat the bleeding operation on the other front wheel all the time making sure the reservoir is not allowed to run low. Then on the left hand rear brake and finally on the right hand rear brake. Finally top up the brake fluid reservoir. When replacing the reservoir cap make sure the air vent is clear.

Notes on Bleeding the Brakes: Use only approved brake fluid. Use clean containers; no trace of mineral oil must be allowed to contaminate the brake fluid or serious brake trouble will ensue. If perfectly clean brake fluid is pumped from the system it may be used for topping up, but such fluid will be aerated and must be allowed to stand undisturbed for 24 hours before re-use.

7.10 Bleeding the Brakes (Dual Line)

Escorts with dual line brakes are fitted with a differential valve and switch unit. This unit can easily be recognised. It is located on the engine compartment rear bulkhead, and five pipes are connected to it. The valve must be held in the centralised position while the bleeding operations are being carried out. If this is not done the brake system warning light will illuminate when the ignition is switched on, thus giving a false indication of a serious fault in the system.

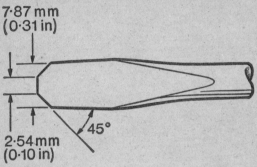

Fig. 33. Tool for centralising piston in differential valve.

A tool is needed to centralise the valve and may be made by filing the end of an old screwdriver to the shape and dimensions shown in Fig. 33. Before commencing to bleed the brakes remove the rubber from the base of the valve unit and insert the tool, to hold the piston in the central position. Remove the tool only when the whole of the bleeding operations have been finally completed. After bleeding the brakes depress and release the brake pedal several times. The system warning light should not illuminate. Depress the test push: the warning light should illuminate. Re-fit the rubber to the unit after removing the centralising tool.

The purpose of the differential valve is to illuminate the warning light if one of the brake lines fails; it is possible otherwise that the driver might be unaware of the failure

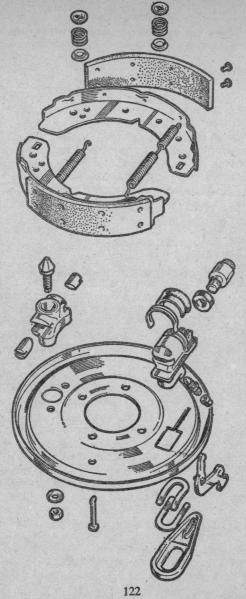

Fig. 34. The rear brake assembly.

since the brakes will still operate, though only on one 'axle'.

The bleeding operations are carried out the same way for dual line brakes as for single line brakes, see 7.9, above but both sections of the fluid reservoir must be topped up as bleeding proceeds.

7.11 How to Remove and Replace Brake Shoes

Rear Brakes: (Look at Fig. 34).

(1) Securely chock the front wheels so that the car cannot move backwards or forwards.

(2) Remove the hub cap and just free the wheel nuts. Jack up the wheel. Remove the wheel nuts and wheel.

(3) Place the handbrake in the fully 'Off' position.

(4) Remove the single slotted screw securing the brake drum to the backplate and pull the drum off the shoes. If the drum is tight, fully release the brake adjuster first, by turning it anti-clockwise.

(5) Each shoe is held against the brake backplate by a small spring and retaining washer located on a spindle in the backplate. To release the spring, depress the washer and after giving it a quarter turn release it. Both spring and washer may then be removed. The spindle will also be released and may be withdrawn from the backplate. The similar parts must be removed from the other brake shoe.

(6) Lift the top shoe and disengage it from the location slots in the operating piston. The handbrake operating cable linkage engages with the leading shoe and may be fitted with a retaining split pin. This pin must be taken out before the shoe can be removed and the springs detached.

When the shoes are removed there is nothing to retain the piston in the cylinder and if left in this condition for any length of time there is risk that the piston may gradually move out of the cylinder, allowing the entry of air and the escape of brake fluid. To prevent this an elastic band should be placed round the cylinder so as to pass over the piston and retain it in position. Alternatively, a piece of soft wire, the ends twisted together to hold it round, will serve the same purpose.

To replace the shoes proceed as explained below:

(1) Make sure the backplate is thoroughly clean. Remove the tappets from the adjuster housing and clean and grease both tappets and housing and replace the tappets. There must be no excess grease left which might contaminate the shoe linings. If the shoe slots are seen not to position properly to receive the shoes when fully home, interchange the tappets in their housings.

(2) Fit the springs to the shoes. The larger spring with the two sets of coils is fitted nearest the expanding cylinder and *on the drum side of the shoes*. The other spring is fitted *on the backplate side of the shoes*. Make sure the lower shoe is connected by the slot on its end to the handbrake link. Hold one shoe in position while the other is pulled to extend the springs and allow the shoe ends to be fitted in their location slots. Before fitting, the shoe ends may be smeared with high melting point grease.

(3) Fit the retaining spindles through the backplate and shoe webs, fit the springs and then the top indented washers. Depress each washer, turn it through 90° and release it. Examine the whole brake assembly carefully, making sure that the shoe ends are all correctly seated and that the shoes are free to move.

(4) Re-fit the brake drum. If difficulty is experienced in fitting the drum, and the brake adjuster was not slacked right off when the drum was removed, this should now be done. With the drum properly in position, fit and tighten the drum securing screw.

(5) Re-fit the wheel and wheel nuts and screw up the nuts after applying the handbrake.

(6) Adjust the brake as explained in 7.4, p. 116.

(7) Lower the wheel to the ground. Check that the wheel nuts are fully tight and re-fit the hub cap.

Front Brake Shoes.

(1) Make sure the handbrake is fully applied.

(2) Remove the hub cap from the wheel on which the shoes are to be removed. Just release the wheel nuts.

(3) Jack up the wheel until it is clear of the ground. Make sure the car is securely supported, using additional support if necessary. Remove the wheel.

(4) Prise off the bearing dust cap. Pull out the split pin

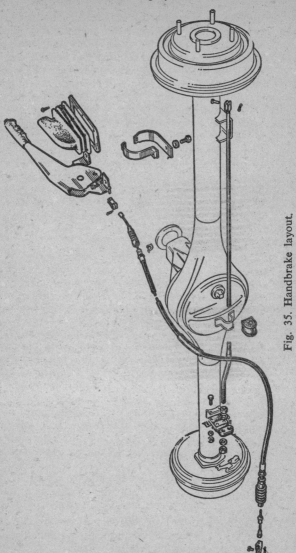

Fig. 35. Handbrake layout.

with a pair of pliers and remove adjuster nut retainer, adjuster nut, thrust washer and bearing cone. Keep the bearing cone free of dirt or dust; protect it carefully.

(5) Withdraw the hub and drum from the spindle. You may need to back off both brake adjusters to facilitate removal.

(6) A clip will be seen on the web of each shoe. These clips are fixed to the ends of the shoe holding spindles and should be removed by pushing them off with a pair of pliers. The spindles may then be withdrawn from the back of the brake plate.

(7) Lift the top shoe and disengage it from the location slots on which the shoe ends rest. As the shoe clears the slots tilt it outwards. Removal of the top shoe also releases the bottom shoe. Remove the springs from the shoes.

To replace the shoes proceed as explained below:

(1) Make sure the face of the backplate is thoroughly clean.

(2) Fully back-off the two brake adjusters, if this has not already been done when removing the drum.

(3) Apply a little high melting point grease to the slots in which the shoe ends locate.

(4) Assemble the two shoes and two springs. The springs should be at the rear of the shoes (hook ends facing outwards). Support the bottom shoe in position while the top shoe is pulled to extend the springs so that its end can be properly located. If any difficulty is experienced in doing this an adjustable spanner may be tightly closed on the lining and lining support near one end and the spanner used as a lever to handle the shoe. The other shoe end may be positioned in the same way. Take great care that the shoe linings are not contaminated by oil or grease.

(5) Fit the shoe holding down spindles from the rear of the backplate, through the shoe webs and press on the retaining clips. Examine the assembly carefully and ensure that the shoes are properly in position and move freely.

(6) Fit the brake drum followed by the bearing cone, thrust washer and bearing adjusting nut. Tighten the

126

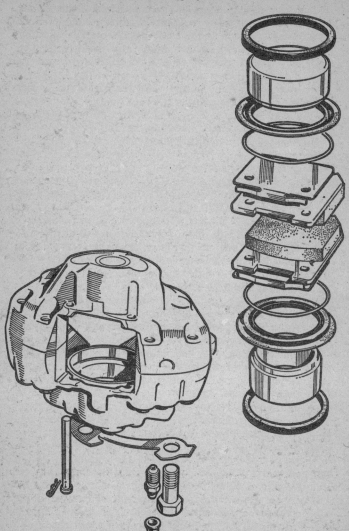

Fig. 36. Front brake—one of the front brake caliper units.

nut to a torque of 27 lb. ft. (3·7 kg.m), rotating the hub while the nut is tightened. Back off the nut by a quarter turn, fit the nut retainer and insert a new split pin. If a torque spanner is not available screw on the adjusting nut as far as possible under light pressure, then apply extra pressure with one hand only on the spanner while the hub is being turned, then turn back and lock as described.

Notes on Re-assembly:

Under no circumstances must the brake pedal be depressed when a brake drum is removed. If this is done there is great risk that the pistons will be pushed out of the wheel cylinders allowing air to enter and brake fluid to escape. If, when the brakes are dismantled, there are signs of fluid leakage this must be remedied before the brakes are re-assembled. When fitting new shoes it is a good idea to fit new pull-off springs also. Do not have both front brakes dismantled at the same time; the intact assembly can then be used as a guide in assembling the other, if any doubt should arise.

7.12 Disc Brake Pad Renewal

The thickness of the friction material on the pads should not be allowed to become thinner than 1/16 in. (0·16 cm). Since these brakes are self adjusting regular inspection is essential. If the metal backing is allowed to contact the brake disc damage will be done that cannot afterwards be remedied by simply fitting new brake pads. Fig. 36 shows the arrangement within the assembly. The pads may be inspected in the caliper opening using a torch or inspection lamp after removal of the wheel. If necessary the pads can be removed for inspection after pulling off the pin retaining clip with a pair of pliers and then withdrawing both pins. The pads themselves are extracted with a pair of pliers. When replacing the pads the friction lining of both must face the brake disc. If new pads are not required the old ones are replaced and the retaining pins and pin locking clips are re-fitted.

If new pads are required make certain that they are of the correct type for your car. Remove the old pads as already described, and then fit the new pads as explained below:

(1) Press each piston a little back into its cylinder. This will cause the fluid in the reservoir to rise, and if it is

already at its normal level it may overflow. It may be necessary therefore to remove some of the fluid from the reservoir. To determine which reservoir is affected in dual line brakes (divided reservoir), press one of the pistons back slightly and note in which reservoir the fluid rises; this is the reservoir it may be necessary to partly empty. Be very careful not to allow the fluid to become contaminated with oil; use only clean and dry containers to hold it.

(2) Fit the new pads with the friction material facing the brake disc.

(3) Fit the shims, one behind each pad.

(4) Fit the pad retaining pins and secure with the locking clips. Make sure all the parts have been correctly fitted.

(5) Operate the brake pedal several times to bring the pads into contact with the brake disc. This will, of course, lower the level in the reservoir and care is needed to make sure it does not fall too low or air will be drawn into the system. Top up as required. With the brakes off, prod the pads with a screwdriver to check that there is slight movement to ensure the pads are free on the retaining pins.

(6) Re-fit the road wheel and screw on the wheel nuts finger tight. Lower the wheel to the ground and fully tighten the wheel nuts.

Notes on Fitting New Pads.

Take great care not to contaminate the pads with oil or grease when fitting them. Make sure the brake disc is quite free from oil or grease.

Any evidence of brake fluid leakage from the caliper unit indicates faulty piston seals. Such a fault must be remedied.

7.13 Rear Brakes Escorts II's (self adjusting)

These brakes are adjusted by the operation of the handbrake. When re-fitting the drum after fitting the shoes the adjusting wheel is backed off. When the drum is re-fitted, operate the handbrake lever continuously until the brakes are properly adjusted. Remove the drum and inspect the shoe linings for wear every 6,000 miles and more frequently when the linings are two-thirds worn.

8

Steering, Wheels and Tyres

8.1 General

The Escort is fitted with rack and pinion steering. The steering wheel is fitted to a shaft which passes through an outer tube which is attached to the engine bulkhead (see Fig. 28, p. 106). The other end of the steering wheel shaft is connected to a flexible coupling which is, in turn, connected to the rack steering assembly drive shaft. Movement of the steering wheel is therefore communicated to the steering assembly.

The rack steering assembly consists of an outer tube, attached by U clips and rubber bushes to the front chassis cross-member. Inside the tube and free to move laterally is a rod on which is machined a rack with teeth suitable to engage with a helical pinion connected to the steering assembly drive shaft.

Each end of the toothed rod or rack is connected via a track rod to the steering arm of one road wheel. Thus, turning the steering wheel turns the rack pinion which then moves the rack; the direction in which the rack moves, and therefore the direction in which the road wheels turn, depends upon the direction in which the steering wheel is turned.

8.2 Fault Symptoms

(1) The car wanders on the road.
(2) Excessive free play in the steering wheel.
(3) Front wheels wobble at high speed.
(4) Front wheels wobble at low speed.
(5) The car pulls continually to one side.
(6) The steering is heavy.

8.3 Causes and Cures

(1) This is usually general wear in the steering resulting in

excessive play at the joints. Make sure that all the tyre pressures are correct and that no steering connections have become slack. Check front and rear suspension carefully, look for weak springs, loose fixings or misalignment. If none of these faults is present have the steering geometry checked.

(2) This is normally due to excessive wear causing slack in the steering joints, see 8.4 below.

(3) This is usually caused by unbalanced front wheels. In turn this may be due to uneven tyre wear. A tyre service station will balance wheels for a small fee. Usually the wobble occurs only within a certain speed range and is not apparent above or below this range. A buckled wheel will cause the trouble. If none of the above faults is present the steering geometry should be checked.

(4) The causes of wheel wobble at low speed are the same as those which cause wobble at high speed, see (3) above.

(5) Check that all tyre pressures are correct. The fault may be caused by incorrect steering geometry, which should be checked with the proper equipment. If the fault only occurs when the brakes are applied, it is due to a brake fault (see 7.2, p. 114).

(6) Soft tyres will cause heavy steering, therefore check the tyre pressures. In models where the steering joints need to be injected with grease (grease nipples fitted), lack of lubrication will result in tightness and cause heavy steering. The steering may be misaligned due to impact damage. The steering column bearings may be incorrectly adjusted—too tight. The fault may be caused by incorrect steering geometry.

8.4 Examination for Wear

Some experience is necessary to check for wear since the amount of wear present will vary considerably with length of service and conditions of use. The presence of *some* wear therefore does not indicate that overhaul is essential. It is possible to detect wear by 'Shaking the joints'. With the road wheels in the 'Straight ahead' position, grasp the rods, one at a time, and attempt to move them lengthwise and sideways. Some slight movement does not indicate excessive wear, and this is where experience is so important. Wear at the steering joint shows as an increase of free play at the steering wheel. There is always some free play in the steering wheel, but this should never be in excess of $1\frac{1}{2}$ in. (39·6 mm). The play is measured by placing the road wheels in the straight ahead position and then gently turning the steering wheel to the limit of its free movement, that is movement before the road wheels commence to turn. When excessive play is present it is worth observing the steering rods and joints while the steering wheel is being turned to move the front wheels.

8.5 Loose Front Wheel Bearings

Loose front wheel bearings will also contribute to free play on the steering wheel, see 8.6 below. It may be that wear has occurred in one or two joints only due to the ingress of dirt and the excessive movements at these joints should be seen. Do not turn the steering wheel violently from lock to lock when checking the steering for wear.

The steering linkage should be checked in a good light, preferably when the car is over a pit or on a ramp. *Do not under any circumstances get underneath the car when it is supported on jacks alone.*

8.6 Front Wheels—Bearing Adjustment

Apply the handbrake. Jack up the wheel on which the bearings are to be adjusted. Make certain that the jack is secure. Remove the wheel, and refer to Fig. 37.

Lever off the dust cap from the end of the stub axle by means of a screwdriver or similar tool. Using a pair of pliers, withdraw the split pin from the locknut and remove the locknut. Tighten the adjusting nut to a torque of 27 lb. ft. while the wheel is being turned by hand. Turn the adjusting nut back a quarter turn. Re-fit the lock nut so that the split pin hole and slots in the nut are aligned, and fit a new split pin and splay out the ends to secure. Finally tap the dust cap back into place. Note that on earlier cars a castellated nut is used as a combined adjusting and locknut. Behind the nut there is a washer with an internal 'pip' which locates in a groove on the shaft threads. To adjust remove the split pin and tighten the nut to 14–17 lb. ft. while turning the wheel then back off the nut a quarter turn. To facilitate the fitting of the split pin two holes are drilled through the hub shaft, one vertical and one horizontal. If none of the holes align with the nut castallations, the nut may be slackened by a very small amount to align one of the holes and thus allow the split pin to be inserted and secured. Do not tighten the nut to align the nut slots with the shaft hole.

Fig. 37. Front hub and bearings.

If the adjustment has to be done without a torque spanner this will be satisfactory if care is exercised. The thing to keep in mind is that there must be some play in the bearings. The right amount of play could be described as 'barely perceptible', but it must be there. It is easier to detect the fine clearance required when the wheel is on and its nuts tightened, by trying to rock the wheel on its bearings. It is important that there should be no brake drag during the adjustment of the bearings.

8.7 Rear Wheel Bearings

The rear wheel bearings are pre-packed with grease and sealed for life, no further lubrication being required.

8.8 Lubrication

The steering joints are all pre-packed with grease during manufacture and require no further lubrication throughout their life. It is necessary to inspect plastic dust covers at intervals because if these become damaged, dirt will enter the bearings and rapid wear will result.

8.9 Punctures

Tubeless tyres do not deflate rapidly when punctured unless the puncture is a very large one, but the object that has penetrated the tyre should be left in position while the car is driven to a convenient place where the puncture can be repaired.

WARNING *Plugged repairs are to be regarded as emergency treatment only.* A proper vulcanized repair (congealed by heat) should be made as soon as possible.

For the interim plugged repair obtain a Dunlop plugging repair kit. This contains rubber solution and a variety of different sizes of rubber plugging strips. A plugging needle is also included in the kit.

Remove the wheel with the punctured tyre and reduce the type pressure to 10 lbs. sq. in. (0·7 kg. sq. cm.) if it is above this pressure. Withdraw the object that caused the puncture. *The tyre should be dry.* Dip the end of the plugging needle in the rubber solution then push the tool through the hole in the tyre. Repeat the insertion several times, dipping the needle each time in the rubber solution. Make sure the edges inside the hole are thoroughly coated with the rubber solution (see Fig. 38).

Select a plug about twice the size of the puncture and insert it in the eye of the plugging needle, so that about a quarter of an inch (6 mm) projects from the eye of the needle. Dip the end of the plugging needle and plug in rubber solution, then push the tool through the puncture hole so that it carries the plug with it. A sudden reduction of the insertion pressure will indicate that the double thickness of insertion plug has passed through the hole. Further movement of the needle will free it from the plug. Finally withdraw the needle and cut off the projecting plug flush with the tyre surface. The tyre can now be inflated to the correct pres-

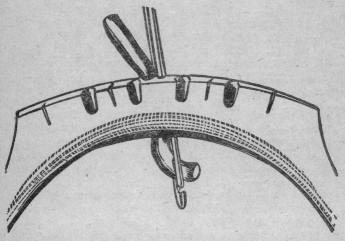

Fig. 38. Repairing a puncture in a tubeless tyre.

sure (see 10.7, p. 145) and the wheel re-fitted. It is sometimes possible to fit a tube to a tubeless tyre, but it is better not to do this without expert advice, otherwise the tyre may chafe the tube and result in sudden blow-out.

8.10 Tyres: General
Tyre wear is closely linked with speed. Continual high speed driving and unnecessarily rapid acceleration greatly increase tyre wear. Excessive use of the brakes shortens tyre life. Tyre life can be prolonged considerably simply by sensible driving.

Do not mix tyres with new and worn treads. Radial ply tyres should be fitted in sets of five (one for the spare wheel). This is because under some circumstances a mixture of cross ply and radial ply tyres can be dangerous. It is permissible to fit a pair of radial tyres to the rear wheels when cross ply tyres are on the front wheels, *but radial tyres on the front wheels only give rise to danger, and such a combination is illegal.* Cross ply and radial ply tyres should not be mixed on the same 'axle'. It is safer not to mix the two different kinds of tyre at all, since this avoids all chance of error.

8.11 Tyre Maintenance

Check the tyres visually every morning for obvious loss of pressure and inflate if necessary. Check the tyre pressures weekly with a tyre pressure gauge when the tyres *are cold* and maintain the correct pressure (see 10.7, p. 145). Inspect the tyres for imbedded flints and other bodies and remove any found.

Do not allow the wheels to strike the kerb ('Kerbing'). Keep the tyres free from oil. Rub any oil from tyres with a petrol-moistened cloth. To obtain even wear interchange the tyres as shown in Fig. 39 *but this only applies if all the tyres are cross-ply or all are radial ply.*

8.12 Fault Symptoms

(1) Tyres wear rapidly.
(2) Tyres become soft—do not retain air over a period.
(3) Tyres wear unevenly.
(4) Burst Cover.
(5) Rapid wear accompanied by 'feathered' edge on tread patterns.

8.13 Causes and Cures

(1) Tyre wear increases rapidly with speed. The rate of tyre wear at 50 m.p.h. (31·2 km.p.h.) is about twice what it is at 30 m.p.h. (18·2 km.p.h). Therefore high speed driving will significantly reduce tyre life. The habit of always rapidly accelerating will result in reduced tyre life. Excessive use of the brakes is also bad. Running with the tyres underinflated will inevitably result in premature tyre failure. A misaligned frame or incorrect steering geometry will cause rapid tyre wear.

(2) Modern inner tubes hold air very well, but after a long period they do need to be topped up. This also applies to tubeless tyres, with which the cars are originally fitted. A quick drop in pressure, or even if it happens overnight, means a puncture. Frequent topping up, say as much as once a week, means that there is either a slow puncture, or with tubeless tyres, possibly a leak.

The tyre valve may be leaking. A valve core can be tested

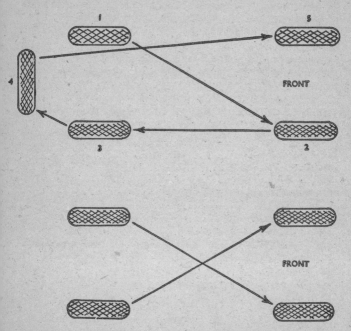

Fig. 39. Changing the wheels to give even tyre wear.

by applying a little soap and water solution to the top of the valve after the cap has been removed. If bubbles appear there is a leak and the valve core should be renewed. If it is necessary to remove a valve core either the wheel must be removed from the car or it must be jacked up so that all weight is removed from it. Otherwise it will be impossible to re-inflate a tubeless tyre, and difficulty may arise even with this precaution. The old valve core can be screwed out, using a special tool and the new valve core replaced with the same tool. The tyre is then immediately re-inflated to the correct pressure (see 10.7, p. 145).

(3) Uneven tread wear is usually due to slack wheel bearings, chassis distortion or to a steering fault. If the front wheel tyres wear unevenly check the hub bearings (see 8.6 earlier) and the steering linkage for wear, see 8.4. Wear on the centre of the tread *only* is caused by excessive pressure, while excessive wear on the tyre shoulders is a sign of under-inflation.

(4) Bursts usually result from damage to the tyre wall caused at some previous time, probably by nipping the tyre on the kerb. Under-inflation will lead to damage to the tyre walls due to excessive flexing causing overheating which may result in a burst.

(5) This effect is evidence of 'scruffing' due to chassis mis-alignment, or incorrect steering geometry.

9
Maintenance

Maintenance is important. Proper maintenance will keep your Escort in good condition, maintain peak performance and the car will last much longer.

Poor maintenance results in reduced performance, brings about avoidable breakdowns and repairs and by doing this it increases the cost of running the car.

The reader is recommended to keep a record of the date and mileage of all services the car receives and the new parts fitted.

The recommended maintenance schedule is given below, broken down into A, B, C, D, E, F maintenance sections, each section being related to the mileage covered or to time periods. The time period is intended to be used when the mileage covered is low. Go by the mileage figures unless the monthly intervals occur first.

Special Note Concerning New and Reconditioned Engines: Before driving check water level in radiator, oil level in engine sump and rocker clearances. Check the cylinder head bolts for tightness after the first 500 miles (800 km.) and recheck the rocker clearances.

On those models fitted with front wheel drum brakes and dual line braking system, service checks are required at half the intervals given for brake servicing in the following maintenance schedules. The service is: front and rear brake adjustment and a check on the operation of the braking system warning light, when this is fitted.

On Escorts not fitted with a crankcase emission valve (early Escorts) the engine oil and oil filter element must be renewed more frequently than the intervals given in the following service schedule. On these models the filter element and engine oil should be renewed every 5000 miles (8000 km.).

The service schedule is set out below:

A MAINTENANCE Daily	D MAINTENANCE First 3,000, then every 6,000 miles
B MAINTENANCE Weekly	E MAINTENANCE First 15,000, then every 18,000 miles
C MAINTENANCE First 600 Miles	F MAINTENANCE at 27,000 miles, then every 30,000 miles

A Maintenance
Daily
Carry out the following checks:
ENGINE: Engine oil level. (See 1.8, p. 25.)
RADIATOR: Water level. (See 3.4, p. 49.)

B Maintenance
Weekly
Carry out the following checks:
BRAKE FLUID RESERVOIR: Check fluid level.
BATTERY: Electrolyte level.
WINDSCREEN WASHER: Water in reservoir.
TYRES: Pressure and condition. (See 10.7, p. 145.)
LIGHTS: Operation of all lights.

C Maintenance
First 600 miles (1,000 km.) or one month.
Carry out the following checks:
ENGINE: Check oil level. (See 1.8, p. 25.)
RADIATOR: Water level. (See 3.4, p. 49.)
BRAKE FLUID RESERVOIR: Fluid level. Maintain level to mark on reservoir wall. On dual system level must be up to bottom of filler neck.
TYRES: Pressure and condition. (See 10.7, p. 145.)
LIGHTS: Operation of all lights.
VALVE ROCKER CLEARANCES: Check clearances. (See 1.10, p. 26.)

CYLINDER HEAD BOLTS: Tightness. (See 10.8, p. 148.)
CARBURETTOR: Idling and mixture setting (2.4, p. 38).
EXHAUST MANIFOLD: Manifold to downpipe bolts. (See 10.8, p. 148.)
ENGINE SUMP BOLTS: Tightness. (See 10.8, p. 148.)
WHEELS: Check nuts for tightness.
Finally road test the car and check for correct brake operation.

D Maintenance

First 3,000 miles (5,000 km.) or at intervals of three months, whichever occurs first, and at each subsequent 6,000 miles (10,000 km.) or at 6 monthly intervals.
Carry out the following checks:
RADIATOR: Water level. (See 3.4, p. 49.)
BRAKE FLUID RESERVOIR: Fluid level.
WINDSCREEN WASHER RESERVOIR: Water level.
ENGINE: Change engine oil and renew filter element. Check for oil or water leakage.
Refer to note at the beginning of this chapter. (See 1.8, 1.9, p. 25.)
DYNAMO: Lubricate rear bearings. (See 4.10, p. 60.) Check mounting bolts for tightness.
SPARKING PLUGS: Clean plugs and re-set gaps or renew plugs. (See 4.40, p. 86 and 10.1, p. 144.)
CONTACT BREAKER: Inspect points, clean or renew as required. (See 4.45, 4.46, p. 89.)
DISTRIBUTOR: Place smear of grease on cam surface. Place two drops of thin oil on pad below rotor. Clean cap.
HT LEADS: Inspect for chafing, clean. Also clean coil if required.
CRANKCASE EMISSION VALVE AND OIL FILLER CAP: Clean. (See 1.17, p. 32.)
CARBURETTOR: Idling/mixture setting, adjust as required. (See 2.4, p. 38.)
VALVE ROCKER CLEARANCES: Adjust clearances, as required. (See 1.10, p. 26.)
RADIATOR: Check for leaks.
COOLING SYSTEM HOSES: Check for leaks and deterioration.
BATTERY: Have battery condition checked for deterioration of leads/connections.

REAR AXLE: Top-up as required. (See 5.12, p. 104.)
REAR SPRING U BOLTS: Check tightness. (See 10.8, p. 148.)
BRAKES: Check disc brake pads for wear (where applicable). (See 7.6, p. 117.) Check brake shoe linings for wear. Examine self-adjusting mechanism and blow clear of dust. Adjust brakes (where necessary). See Chapter 7. Inspect braking system for leakage and chafing hoses.
EXHAUST SYSTEM: Check for condition.
FUEL PUMP: Clean filter. (At first 3,000 miles only.)
GEARBOX: Change oil. (At first 3,000 miles otherwise top up only.)
WHEELS: Check nuts for tightness.
FAN BELT: Check tension and condition. (See 3.5, p. 50.)
SUSPENSION: Check all around for wear.
STEERING: Check linkage for wear. Inspect ball joint covers. If in doubt as to condition consult nearest Ford dealer.
CLUTCH: Inspect clutch cable and adjust if required. (See 5.6, p. 100.)
LIGHTS, INSTRUMENTS AND CONTROLS: Check that all lights, instruments and controls operate correctly.
HANDBRAKE LINKAGE: Lubricate linkage and adjust if required. (See 7.7, p. 117.)
SEAT BELTS: Check for security.
TYRES: Check pressures and tyre condition. (See 10.7, p. 145.) Interchange if required to even out wear.
Check for uneven wear as evidence of wheel misalignment.
MISCELLANEOUS: Lubricate door locks, lock cylinders, door striker wedge, door check stops, bonnet safety catch pivot. All oil can points, and accelerator cable linkage.
(AUTOMATIC TRANSMISSION): Top up. (See 5.11, p. 104.)
Road test car and check for correct brake operation.

E Maintenance
First 15,000 miles (25,000 km) or at interval of 15 months. Then every 18,000 miles (30,000 km.) or at interval of 18 months. Repeat D Maintenance and add the following:
BRAKE SERVO: Renew servo air filter (when servo brakes are fitted).
AIR CLEANER ELEMENT: Change element. (See 2.9, p. 44.)

IGNITION TIMING: Check. (See 4.49, p. 90.)

F Maintenance

Carry out D Maintenance plus the following:

27,000 miles (45,000 km.) and each subsequent 30,000 miles (50,000 km.).

FRONT WHEEL BEARINGS: Clean, re-pack with grease and re-adjust. (See 8.6, p. 132.)

At 39,000 miles (65,000 km.) the brake hoses should be carefully examined. In general, at this mileage it is advisable to renew all the rubbers in the braking system and to fill the system with new fluid. Refer to a Ford Agent for advice if you are in doubt.

The trend is to cut down maintenance because of its cost when it has to be paid for. However, frequent and careful inspection plus extra maintenance on the part of the do-it-yourself motorist pays dividends. The latest Escort II range servicing schedule is given below, additional to daily and weekly checks already mentioned:

Every 6,000 miles (9,600 km).

Renew engine oil and filter.

Check ignition timing.

Check/renew spark plugs as required.

Contact breaker points gap check/adjust/renew points as required.

Check carburettor idling adjustment.

Check/adjust fan drive belt.

Check/adjust valve clearances.

Check brake pads and shoe linings (self-adjusting brakes) for wear.

Adjust brakes where adjustment is provided.

Check gearbox oil level. Top up as required.

Check rear axle oil level. Top up as required.

Check clutch adjustment.

Renew air cleaner element.

Check exhaust system.

Check steering linkage.

Lubricate all locks and fittings.

Adjust handbrake linkage.

Check dynamo/alternator mounting bolts. Lubricate dynamo, if fitted.

Lubricate throttle linkage and adjust, if required.

Check lights.

Every 36,000 miles (57,000 km).

Remove, clean, re-pack with grease, re-fit and adjust front wheel bearings.

10
General Data

10.1 Sparking Plugs

The recommended make and type of sparking plug is Auto-lite AG.22, for all of the first range of models. These are 14 mm plugs. The correct points gap is 0·025 in. (0·64 mm). Escort II's, AG22, gap 0·030 in. (0·75 mm) ; 1600 Ghia GT only, AGR12. Equivalent plugs of other make may be used.

10.2 Battery

The battery is of the lead acid type, 6 cell, 12 volt. The negative battery terminal is earthed. The standard battery has a capacity of 32 ampere hours at a 20 hours discharge rate. The electrolyte specific gravity when the battery is fully charged is 1·275 to 1·290.

10.3 Contact Breaker

The distributor cam rotates anti-clockwise, looking down on the rotor. Spark advance is automatically controlled by the centrifugal action of rotating weights and the induction manifold suction. The points gap is 0·025 in. (0·64 mm).

10.4 Cylinder Firing Order

The cylinder firing order is 1, 2, 4, 3. No. 1 cylinder being the one nearest the radiator.

10.5 Capacities

Fuel tank: 9·0 Imp. Gallons, 10·8 U.S. Gallons (40·9 Litres)

Cooling system: 9·0 Imp. Pints, 10·8 U.S. Pints (5·2 Litres), with heater. 7·90 Imp. Pints, 9·48 U.S. Pints (4·98 Litres) without heater.

Engine sump: 6·4 Imp. Pints (7·6 U.S. Pints (3·6 Litres) including filter. Filter capacity ⅔ Imp. Pint, 0·8 U.S. Pint (0·38 Litres).

Rear axle differential: 2 Imp. Pints, 2·4 U.S. Pints (1·1 Litres).

Gearbox (Manual): 1·5 Imp. Pints, 1·9 U.S. Pints (0·90 Litres).

Gearbox (Automatic) including torque converter: 11¼ Imp. Pints, 13 U.S. Pints (6·39 Litres).

Steering: 0·25 Imp. Pint, 0·3 U.S. Pint (0·15 Litre).

10.6 Cooling System

For capacity, see 10.5. Thermostat wax type located in cylinder head. Commences to open 85° to 89°C (185° to 192°F). Fully open 98° to 102°C (210° to 216°F).

The system is pressurised to increase operating temperature and therefore improve engine efficiency. Valves are located in the radiator cap which maintain a pre-determined pressure in the system when the water is at normal operating temperature and to prevent excessive external pressure, due to partial vacuum, when the system cools. The pressure in the system when the engine is at normal operating temperature is 13 p.s.i. (0·91 kg.sq.cm.).

Fan Drive Belt Tension: The total free movement in the belt at the mid point between the generator and fan pulley should be ½ in. (1·3 cm) when the dynamo fixings are tight.

CAUTION: If the radiator cap is removed when the engine is hot the release of pressure in the cooling system will cause the water to suddenly boil and steam and water to be ejected. Therefore if it is necessary to remove the radiator cap before the engine has cooled, you should first cover it with a heavy cloth and turn the cap *slowly* anti-clockwise. In this way the pressure is gradually released and the ejection of steam and water avoided.

10.7 Tyres

The tyre pressures in the table apply only to cars fitted with standard wheels and the tyre sizes and types listed. The information is the latest available.

The conditions of use are:

A. Normal—only one or two passengers, little or no luggage, speed below 70 m.p.h.

B. Fully Laden—4 or 5 passengers and luggage, or luggage, equivalent in weight to 4 or 5 passengers. Speed below 70 m.p.h.

C. High Speed—These pressures to be used for sustained high speed, one hour or more at above 70 m.p.h. in countries where this is permissible.

D. Fully Laden High Speed—Sustained high speed (above 70 m.p.h.) with full or high complement of passengers and/or luggage.

Check and adjust the tyre pressures when the tyres are cold.

Do not fit radial ply tyres to some of the wheels: all tyres should be radial or cross ply.

For a half loaded van the rear tyre pressures should be 32 PSI (2·3). It is important to maintain the correct tyre pressures, this ensures maximum tyre life and gives optimum vehicle control and safety.

10.8 Tyre Pressures, Escort II models.

These vary according to wheel size and load, throughout the range:

Wheel size	type	Normal Load	Full Load
6.00×12	cross-ply	F.22 p.s.i. (1.5 kg. sq. cm.)	F.24 (1.7)
		R.27 p.s.i. (1.9 kg. sq. cm.)	R.30 (2.1)
155×12	radial	F.22 p.s.i. (1.5 kg. sq. cm.)	F.24 (1.7)
		R.27 p.s.i. (1.9 kg. sq. cm.)	R.36 (2.5)
155×13	radial	F.22 p.s.i. (1.5 kg. sq. cm.)	F.24 (1.7)
		R.24 p.s.i. (1.7 kg. sq. cm.)	R.36 (2.5)
175/70×13	radial	F.22 p.s.i. (1.5 kg. sq. cm.)	F.24 (1.7)
		R.24 p.s.i. (1.7 kg. sq. cm.)	R.28 (2.0)

For sustained high speed driving above 80 m.p.h. it is recommended to raise these pressures all round by 3 p.s.i. (0.2 kg. sq. cm.).

Model	Tyre Type and Size	Tyre pressures (tyres cold) in PSI. Figures in brackets—kg. sq. cm. Conditions of Use							
		A		B		C		D	
		Front	Rear	Front	Rear	Front	Rear	Front	Rear
1100 c.c.	5.50×12 Cross Ply	24 (1.7)	24 (1.7)	24 (1.7)	30 (2.0)	28 (2.0)	28 (2.0)	28 (2.0)	30 (2.1)
1300 c.c.	155×12 Radial Ply	24 (1.7)	28 (2.0)	24 (1.7)	28 (2.0)	24 (1.7)	28 (2.0)	24 (1.7)	28 (2.0)
GT	155SR×12 Radial Ply	24 (1.7)	28 (2.0)	24 (1.7)	28 (2.0)	24 (1.7)	28 (2.0)	24 (1.7)	28 (2.0)
Estate Car 1100 c.c.	600×12 Cross Ply	24 (1.7)	24 (1.7)	24 (1.7)	30 (2.1)	28 (2.0)	28 (2.0)	28 (2.0)	30 (2.1)
1300 c.c.	155×12 Radial Ply	24 (1.7)	28 (2.0)	24 (2.7)	28 (2.0)	24 (1.7)	28 (2.0)	24 (1.7)	28 (2.0)
6 cwt. Van	5.50×12 Light Van	24 (1.7)	24 (1.7)	24 (1.7)	43 (3.0)	28 (2.0)	28 (2.0)	—	—
8 cwt. Van	6.00×12 Light Van	24 (1.7)	24 (1.7)	24 (1.7)	43 (3.0)	28 (2.0)	28 (2.0)	—	—

10.8 Torque Ratings

The tightening torques below are in pound-feet (lb/ft).

Wheel nuts	50 to 65
Front wheel bearing adjusting nut	(See 8.6, p. 132.)
Rear brake backplate to axle	15 to 18
Hydraulic unions	7 to 8
Bleed valves	5 to 7
Differential filler plug	25 to 30
Shock absorber to mounting bracket	25 to 30
Shock absorber to spring plate	25 to 30

The shock absorber attachment nuts must be tightened when the weight of the car is on the wheels.

*Rear spring U bolts	18 to 26
*Rear spring front attachment eye bolt	25 to 30
*Rear spring shackles	8 to 10

These must not be finally tightened until the weight of the car is on the wheels.

Manifolds, nuts and bolts	65 to 70
Sump screws	7 to 9
Oil pump	12 to 15
Oil filter centre retaining bolt	12 to 15
Rocker cover	2·5 to 3·5
Cylinder head bolts	65 to 70
Sump drain plug	20 to 25
Exhaust manifold clamp (Brass nuts)	7 to 10
Exhaust manifold clamp (Steel nuts)	15 to 20
Exhaust U clamp bolt	12 to 15
Water pump	5 to 7
Thermostat housing	12 to 15
Fan blade	5 to 7
Rocker shaft	25 to 30

10.9 Weights

2 door de luxe	1762 lb.
2 door super	1775 lb.
4 door de luxe	1806 lb.
4 door super	1819 lb.
2 door estate car	1920 lb.
6 cwt van	1653 lb.
8 cwt van	1718 lb.

When automatic transmission is fitted add 33 lb.

10.10 Steering Geometry

Toe-in	0.0 to 0.25 in
Castor	0.35' to 1° 35' (standard)
	0° 40' to 1° 40' (heavy duty)
Camber	0° 10' 1° 10' (standard)
	0° 50' to 1° 50' (heavy duty)
Turning circle, saloon and estate car	29 ft.
Turning circle, van	29.7 ft.

10.11 Valve Timing

The valve timing for all engines (except GT) is:

Inlet valve commences to open	23° BTDC
Inlet valve commences to close	53° ABDC
Exhaust valve commences to open	53° BTDC

10.12 Ignition Timing

Model	Compression Ratio	Fuel octane rating	Initial spark Advance
1100 cc. and all	9 : 1	97	6°
Escort II models	9 : 1	94	2°
except 1600 GT	8 : 1	89	10°
	8 : 1	86	10°
1300 c.c.	9 : 1	97	10°
	9 : 1	94	6°
	8 : 1	89	10°
	8 : 1	86	4°
GT	9 : 2	97	10°
GT 1600	9 : 1	97	10°

10.13 Dynamo

	Lucas Type C.40	Lucas C-40L
Maximum current	22 amps	25 amps
Maximum output (power)	264 watts	300 watts
Drive belt tension	Both types ½ in. (13 mm)	

10.14 Starter Motor

Inertia Engagement Type:

Current at zero RPM	340 amps at 7·4 volts
Current draw at 1,000 starter RPM	245 amps at 7·8 volts
Torque with starter shaft locked	6.4 lb. ft.

10.15 Engine Oil Pressure

The normal operating oil pressure on all models is 35 to 40 PSI (2·46 to 2·81 kg.sq.cm). The GT model is fitted with an oil pressure gauge. The oil pressure may drop to 5-7 PSI (0·35 to 0·4 kg.sq.cm) when the engine is running at idling speed.

10.16 Distributor

The distributor cam rotates anti-clockwise, looking down on the rotor. The distributors fitted to the various models are not interchangeable and if it becomes necessary to fit a new distributor a Ford Agent must be consulted to ensure a correct replacement.

10.17 Rocker Clearances

The rocker clearances are the same for all models. The clearance between each exhaust valve and its rocker when the engine is hot should be 0·020 in. (0·50 mm). The clearance between each inlet valve and its rocker when the engine is hot should be 0·10 in. (0·25 mm). (For instructions on how to adjust the rocker/valve clearance see 1.10, p. 26.)

Escorts II models: All engines: when cold. Inlet 0·008 in. (20 mm). Exhaust 0·022 in. (0·56 mm). Check and adjust clearances a minimum of 5 minutes after stopping the engine.

10- 8 Approved Lubricants and Brake Fluid

Front wheel bearings .	Lithium base grease
Distributor	Engine oil
Steering gear	SAE 90 EP gear oil
Dynamo rear bearing	Engine oil
Automatic transmission	Ford M-2C33-F or Castrol TQF
Brake fluid reservoir	Ford ME-3833-F
	Castrol-Girling brake fluid
General greasing	Lithium base grease with 1% molybdenum disulphide
	Ford EMIC-3 or Castrol MS3

Engine oil: The lubricants listed below are recommended for use in the United Kingdom only. Where very high or low temperatures obtain a different range of lubricants is required.

Castrol	Castrol GTX (This is an 'All Season' 20W-50 oil suitable for temperatures down to 25° F)
Esso	Esso Motor Oil 20W
	Esso Extra 10W-30 or Uniflow
	Esso Extra 20W-50

Mobil	Mobiloil Super 10W-50
	Mobiloil Special 20W-50
Texaco	Regent Havoline 20-20W
	Regent Havoline 10W-30
	Regent Havoline 20W-50
Shell	Shell Super 101 (10W-30)
	Shell Super 100 (20W-30)
BP	BP Super Visco Static 10W-40
	BP Super Visco Static 20W-50
Fina	Fina Supergrade 10W-30
	Fina Supergrade 20W-50

Approved gearbox and rear axle lubricants:

	Gearbox	Rear Axle
Castrol	Castrol Hypoy Light	Castrol Hypoy
Esso	Esso Gear Oil EP 80	Esso Gear Oil GP 90/140
Mobil	Mobilube GX 80	Mobilube GX 90
Texaco	Regent Multi-Gear Oil EP 80	Regent Multi-gear Oil EP 90
Shell	Shell Spirax EP 80	Shell Spirax EP 90
BP	BP Gear Oil SAE 80 EP	BP Gear Oil 90 EP
Fina	Fina Pontonic MP SAE 80	MP SAE 90 Fina Pontonic

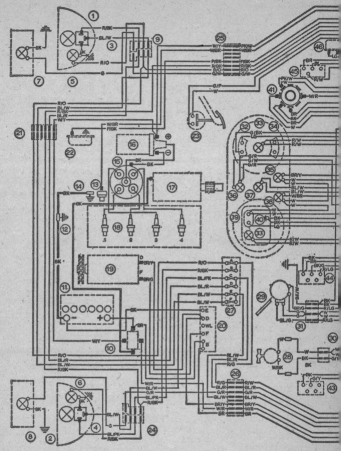

Wiring Colour Code:

R	Red	BR Brown	P Purple
BK	Black	G Green	O Orange
BL	Blue	Y Yellow	PK Pink
W	White	LG Light Green	

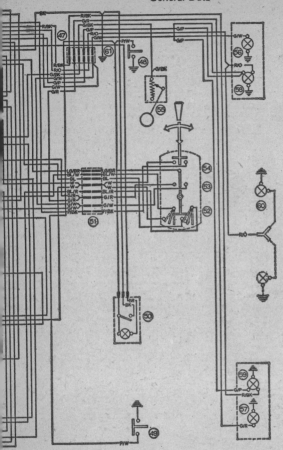

Fig. 40. Wiring diagram—Super Saloon, R.H.D.

Where more than one colour is used to identify the cable, it is shown on the diagram accordingly, BR/G signifying Brown/Green, R/BK, Red/Black, G/Y green/yellow and so on.

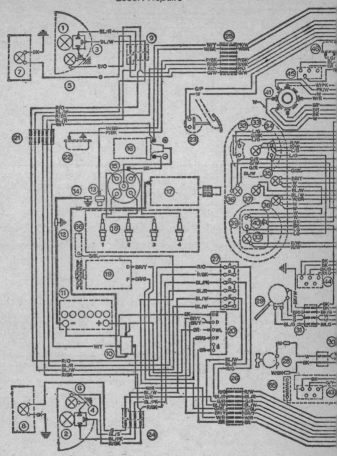

Wiring Colour Code:

R Red	BR Brown	P Purple
BK Black	G Green	O Orange
BL Blue	Y Yellow	PK Pink
W White	LG Light Green	

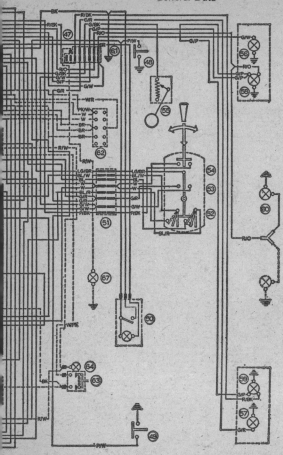

Fig. 41. Wiring diagram—De luxe Saloon, Estate Car and Van (R.H.D.).

Where more than one colour is used to identify the cable, it is shown on the diagram accordingly, BR/G signifying Brown/Green, R/BK, Red/Black, G/Y green/yellow and so on.

WIRING DIAGRAMS KEY
Applies to Fig. 40 and Fig. 41

1. R.H. headlamp.
2. L.H. headlamp.
3. R.H. headlamp connector.
4. L.H. headlamp connector.
5. R.H. sidelamp (front).
6. L.H. sidelamp (front).
7. R.H. direction indicator lamp (front).
8. L.H. direction indicator lamp (front).
9. R.H. lighting connector (front).
10. Starter solenoid.
11. Battery.
12. Body earth.
13. Oil pressure sender unit.
14. Engine earth.
15. Distributor.
16. Ignition coil.
17. Starter motor.
18. Sparking plugs.
19. Dynamo.
20. Regulator.
21. L.H. to R.H. loom connector
22. Horn.
23. Brake light switch.
24. L.H. lighting connector (front).
25. R.H. bulkhead multi-way connector (front).
26. L.H. bulkhead multi-way connector.
27. Fuses.
28. Heater motor.
29. Windscreen wiper motor.
30. Heater motor connector.
31. Windscreen wiper motor connector.
32. Fuel gauge.
33. Panel light.
34. Temperature gauge.
35. Dynamo warning light.
36. Direction indicator lamp.
37. Main beam indicator lamp.
38. Oil pressure warning lamp.
39. Instrument voltage stabiliser.
40. Instrument earth.
41. Ignition switch.
42. Oil pressure gauge.
43. Heater motor switch.
44. Windscreen wiper switch.
45. Head/side lamp switch.
46. Flasher unit.
47. Rear loom connector.
48. R.H. courtesy light switch.
49. L.H. courtesy light switch.
50. Interior light switch.
51. Headlamp/flasher, direction indicator and horn switch connector.
52. Headlamp flasher switch.
53. Director indicator switch.
54. Horn switch.
55. Fuel gauge sender unit.
56. R.H. direction indicator lamp (rear).
57. L.H. direction indicator lamp (rear).
58. R.H. stop/sidelamp (rear).
59. L.H. stop/sidelamp (rear).
60. Rear number plate lamp.
61. Body earth.
62. Ignition lock.
63. Cigar lighter.
64. Cigar lighter illumination lamp.
65. Heater motor resistor (two speed).
66. Water temperature sender unit.
67. Battery condition indicator unit.
68. Tachometer.
69. Water temperature gauge.
70. Automatic transmission illuminating lamp.

Some of the components listed are not shown on both diagrams.

INDEX

V

W